HAWORTH

'A strange uncivilized little place'

HAWORTH

'A strange uncivilized little place'

STEVEN WOOD

TEMPUS

Dedicated with love and gratitude to my mother Stella Ingham and my wife Lynn Wood.

Frontispiece: This unusual photograph shows part of Haworth Main Street as it was in the 1870s. A linen draper's shop is visible on the left. The two white cottages in the centre were to be demolished around 1880 – they represent a kind of eighteenth-century housing which would once have been common in the village but which is now rare.

First published 2005

Tempus Publishing Limited
The Mill, Brimscombe Port,
Stroud, Gloucestershire, GL5 2QG
www.tempus-publishing.com

British Library Cataloguing in Publication Data.
A catalogue record for this book is available from the British Library.

ISBN 0 7524 3508 6

Typesetting and origination by Tempus Publishing Limited.
Printed in Great Britain.

Contents

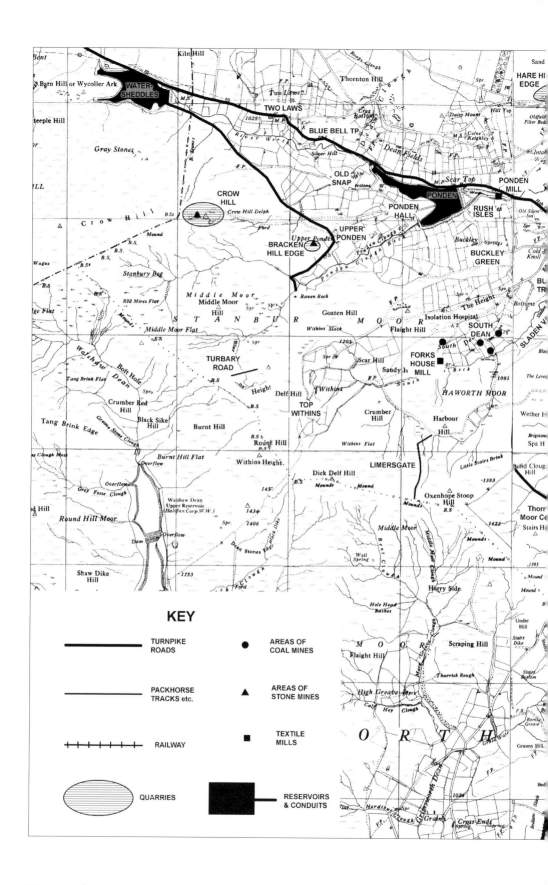

KEY

━━━	**TURNPIKE ROADS**	●	**AREAS OF COAL MINES**
───	**PACKHORSE TRACKS etc.**	▲	**AREAS OF STONE MINES**
┼┼┼┼┼┼┼	**RAILWAY**	■	**TEXTILE MILLS**
(oval)	**QUARRIES**	(black shape)	**RESERVOIRS & CONDUITS**

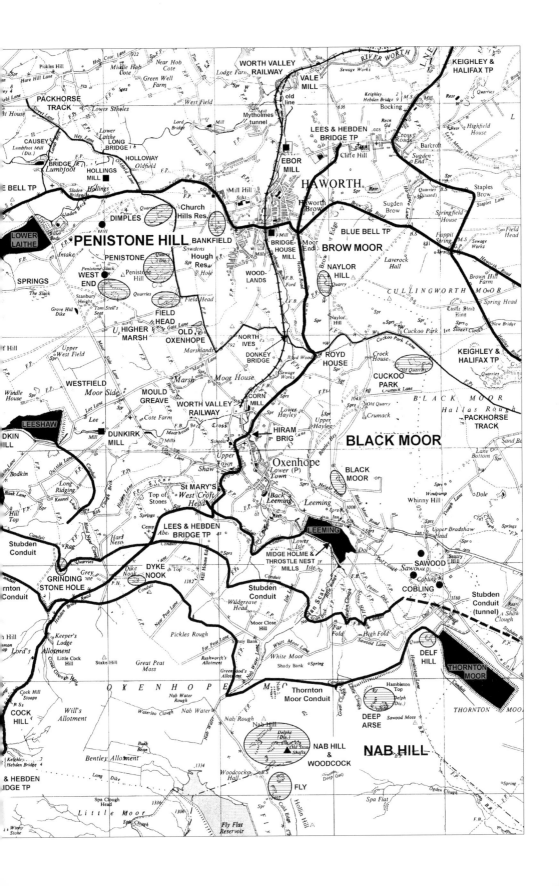

Preface

The book's sub-title is taken from a letter which Charlotte Brontë wrote to her publisher in 1849. A member of the company was due to call at Haworth to collect the manuscript of *Shirley* and Charlotte wrote: 'He will find Haworth a strange uncivilized little place such as – I dare say – he never saw before.' Not the most enthusiastic account of her moorland home perhaps, but positively affectionate compared with the following damning judgement from a writer in the *Nelson Leader* in 1906: 'There is little in Haworth to interest the visitor … take away the Brontës from Haworth and you have practically nothing left.' I hope to show in these pages that this latter view is quite false (even if there might have been a little truth in Charlotte's view of the place). Haworth, with or without the Brontës, is a fascinating village and richly repays any time devoted to the study of its past.

When I first moved up the Worth Valley from my original home in Keighley I had innumerable questions about Haworth and the surrounding area to which no one seemed to have the answers. I have now spent twenty years trying to find the answers to these questions.

What follows is a very brief look at some aspects of the Haworth area. The focus is mainly on the village of Haworth but I have used examples from other parts of the township where necessary.

A few terms should be defined at the outset. Haworth village was the main focus of the Township or Chapelry of Haworth which consisted of four hamlets – Haworth, Stanbury, Near Oxenhope and Far Oxenhope. Of these, Haworth formed one manor and the two Oxenhopes another. Stanbury remained a part of the Manor of Bradford – the 'Manor of Stanbury' being a legal fiction.

In order to cover as much ground as possible without being superficial I have used one or two detailed examples in each chapter to stand for the greater whole. I hope this will explain, if not excuse, any apparent imbalance in treatment. Inevitably some readers will regret the omission of certain things and wonder at the space devoted to others.

Haworth Village in 1879.

The first eight chapters cover the ways in which Haworth earned its living (Chapters 1-3), its communications (Chapter 4), the reservoirs and gas works (Chapter 5) and the most important components of the village itself (Chapters 6-8). The remaining two chapters are more or less independent examinations of some popular beliefs (Chapter 9) and some less well known aspects of the Brontës' connections with Haworth (Chapter 10).

Note on the text: Sums of money are quoted throughout in pre-decimal currency. To take an example, £1 2s 6d is read as 'one pound, two shillings and sixpence'.

Previous pages: Map of Haworth Township showing quarries, mills, reservoirs, roads and other places mentioned in the text. Base map reproduced from 1946/7 Ordnance Survey maps.

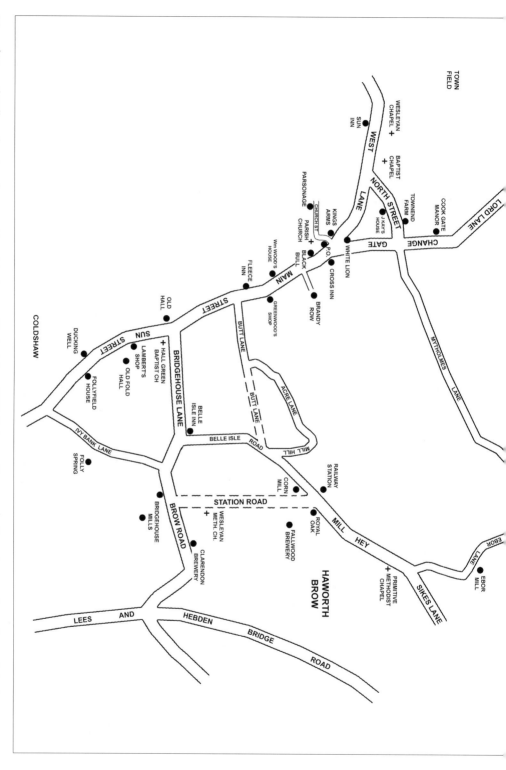

Map of Haworth Village showing places mentioned in the text. Derived from 1852 Ordnance Survey map. Some later roads are shown dashed.

Acknowledgements

Over the past two decades I have accumulated debts of gratitude to a great many people. I am grateful to all those local people who have lent me photographs and documents, allowed me to look at their properties or otherwise provided information. I gladly record my particular indebtedness to the following individuals: Michael Baumber, Robin Greenwood and Reg Hindley have generously shared the fruits of their own extensive researches into the area. All of them kindly read the manuscript and provided much sound guidance, for which I am grateful. The manuscript was also read at various stages by Gordon Crowther, John Debarr and Lynn Wood – they have saved me from making many errors.

I am indebted to the following for information on particular topics: John Batty and Ken Golisti on the gas works, Cedric Gilson and Ronnie Mace on quarrying, Eddie Kelly on pubs and breweries, Arnold Pacey and many other members of the Yorkshire Vernacular Buildings Study Group on buildings, David Pearson and Ralph Povey on the railway and Peter Ward of Yorkshire Water on the reservoirs. I am indebted to Ann Dinsdale, the Brontë Society's librarian, whose help went far beyond the specific assistance she has given on matters relating to the Brontës and their associates. Many of these experts also read relevant parts of the first draft for me. Cathleen McRae's comments here were also valuable.

Topographical history of this kind requires a detailed knowledge of the place. This can only be acquired by walking extensively with informed and observant people. I have been lucky to do much of my walking with Jack Cuthbert, John Debarr and Reg Hindley – they have all contributed much.

I also wish to record my appreciation of the companionship and help of all the members of the old Haworth Local History Group, the new Upper Worth Valley History Group, the Haworth Historians' Dining Club, the Pennine Field Group and Reg Hindley's WEA Worth Valley Walks course. The custodians of the archives have (with rare exceptions) been courteous and helpful. My thanks go to all the staff, present and past, of: Bradford, Keighley, Halifax and Leeds Local Studies Libraries; the Brontë Parsonage Museum; the Bradford, Leeds and Wakefield offices of the West Yorkshire Archive Service (WYAS); the House of Lords Record Office; and to Jens Hislop, custodian of the Haworth parish church records. In particular my debt to Irene McNamara of Keighley Local Studies Library is vast. Dr Ian Dewhirst MBE was an inspirational reference librarian at Keighley for many years – I owe him a great deal.

All remaining errors of fact, perversities of interpretation and infelicities of style are entirely the author's responsibility.

Finally I would like to thank Bob Duckett who suggested that I should write this book; thanks also to David Buxton and Emily Pearce at Tempus for all their help.

For permission to reproduce photographs I am indebted to the following: the Brontë Society's library [BS], Robert Buckley (for the photographs of his late father-in-law Harold Horsman – a hugely talented photographer) [HH], Ian Dewhirst [ID], John and Barbara Laycock (who have also given much other help over the years) for photographs from the collection of the late Jack Laycock [TJL], Ronnie Mace [RM], Miles Marsden [MM], Eric Stoney [ES] and my friend and neighbour Bill Parker [WEP]. Jack Kay's portrait is reproduced by kind permission of Christine Rose [CR]. The collections of photographs held at Keighley Local Studies Library have been of primary importance [KLS]. All my own photographs are credited SCW. The acknowledgements due for each illustration are indicated in the captions using the abbreviations indicated here in square brackets.

My plan of Springs Farm is based on work done by Alison Armstrong and Arnold Pacey.

The map of Woodcock Quarry comes from the Bradford office of WYAS. Other illustrations are from the author's own collection.

The maps of the Ordnance Survey are an unparalleled national treasure and I am happy to acknowledge the use I have made of extracts from the 1:25000 sheets SD93 of 1946 and SE03 of 1947.

Steven Wood
Haworth, 2004

one

Farming

Yorkshire has large areas of fertile arable land but they lie to the east of the Pennine foothills. The hill country of the West Riding does not readily support crop growing and is largely given over to rough pasture. The Millstone Grit and its associated shales make respectively for light sandy or heavy clay soils. Where the two types mix, a reasonable loamy soil can result but all these soils are deficient in lime. These conditions combine with rather low average temperatures and high rainfall (typically 50 inches a year or more on the higher land) to make for difficult agricultural conditions. The use which has been made of this unpromising land has, of course, varied over time as the inhabitants' needs have changed. In medieval and early modern times there would have been much more need to approach self-sufficiency and grain would have been grown. It seems likely that a hardy variety of oats would have been the principal grain crop, and porridge and oat cake remained staples of the area's diet into the twentieth century. A very few field names suggest that wheat may have been grown at times in Haworth Township but it cannot have been easy to do. Apart from oats it is likely that root crops were grown both for human and animal consumption.

There is a tendency to associate the moors with sheep grazing although Haworth lies outside the main sheep farming area of the Craven dales. Sheep have certainly been kept, and continue to be kept, on the Haworth moors. Although sheep farming requires little in the way of dedicated buildings, some traces of its presence in the past do remain. One or two place names (Sheep Cote Swamp and Jarnel Washfold), the occasional fold, a couple of shepherds in the mid-nineteenth century census returns and the fact that sheep were a considerable item of freight on the Worth Valley Railway line all attest to at least some sheep farming in the township. There tends to be an assumption that if an area has both sheep and textile making there must be a direct connection. In fact the wool of local sheep, the hardy Lonks, is not suitable for worsted production. Wool for worsteds was obtained from Leicestershire, Lincolnshire and the Cheviots. Most manufacturers would buy their wool through a wool stapler. Wool staplers sorted their

Sheep-shearing at Springs Farm, 1915. [KLS]

fleeces so that the manufacturer could buy just the quality of wool that he required. Staplers, by extending credit to the manufacturers, were also important sources of finance. Local wool may well have been used to make coarse woollen cloths in the medieval period but after that any sheep raised would have been principally for meat rather than wool. It seems that a number of farms with moorland runs did keep sheep but how important they were in local agriculture is uncertain. What does seem clear is that the small farms of the area were mainly concerned with dairy cattle with a little arable in the form of oats and root crops.

The 1851 census returns show that there were about 220 farmers in Haworth Township at that time. Of these almost half had a second occupation – most were wool-combers, handloom weavers or quarrymen. The rest were mainly grocers, butchers, inn keepers, carriers and clog- and shoe-makers. As well as the farmers themselves there were about thirty farm labourers and over a hundred wives and older children of farmers who were involved in farm work.

The census returns and tithe award also give us a good idea of the size of these farms. The total amount of farmland in the township was about 5,000 acres. There was a negligible amount of arable land (120 acres), a quarter of the cultivated land was hay meadow and three quarters was pasture. No farm was larger than 150 acres and most were between ten and fifty acres in extent. Twenty-six farms were less than ten acres.

The growth of Haworth village in the later nineteenth century has obscured its essentially rural nature. In the eighteenth and nineteenth centuries there were farms in the middle of the village.

An estate map of 1769 shows that the village was completely surrounded by farmland and that there were at least seven farms in the village itself. Three of these were amongst the farms which held strips of land in the Town Field – a clear relic of open-field farming from the Middle Ages. These strips persisted well into the nineteenth century and, seen from Oakworth in the evening light, are still quite apparent today. It is not clear whether there was a full-blown three-field system in operation in Haworth, but there is sufficient evidence from field names and other sources that there was a fair amount of arable open field in Haworth, Oxenhope and Stanbury.

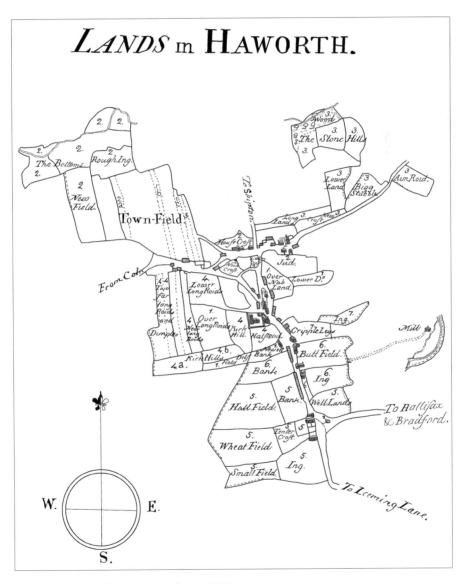

Map of Haworth Village, redrawn from a 1769 estate map.

The Town Field showing medieval open field strips. [SCW]

A full history of agriculture in the Haworth area is still wanting and requires much work, but one farm has been the subject of a detailed historical study and will serve as an example of a typical small farm. Visitors walking to the Brontë waterfalls generally park near the Lower Laithe reservoir and walk the farm track along Enfieldside. The first farm building to be passed is Springs which, until recently, was in ruins but is now splendidly restored as a private dwelling. When the water board sold the ruin for conversion the opportunity was taken to make a detailed survey of the buildings and a related study of historical sources. From these a fairly full picture of this little farm has emerged.

Springs is what is often referred to as a laithe house – one in which the house and barn are under a single roof but in which the animal and human accommodation are separate. The house consists of two ground floor and two first floor rooms with a single-storey lean-to building at the east end. The lean-to housed a wash kitchen and, probably, a privy. The wash kitchen contained a set pot for heating water and there would probably have been a shallow stone sink as well.

From the wash kitchen a door opens into the first of the two ground floor rooms. This was oak beamed and was heated by a nineteenth-century fireplace. A small keeping cellar lies under this room with stone shelves for food storage. Notches in the rafters show that at one time there was a handloom fitted in this room near the four-light window. The second room was entered

Springs Farm, *c.* 1905. [MM]

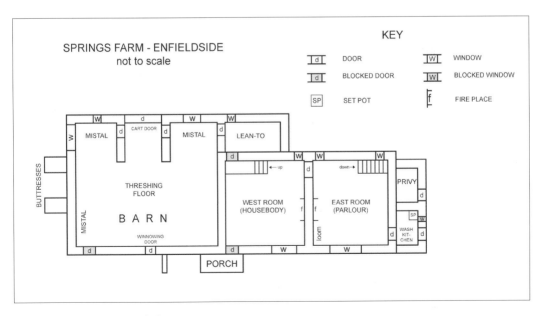

Plan of Springs Farm before restoration.

by a doorway beside the fireplace and contained a small range for cooking and water heating. A small sink was situated under the window. There is some indication that these two rooms were originally subdivided to provide a dairy at the back of the house. The first floor had two bedrooms, each with a fireplace. All four rooms were lit by mullioned windows.

Beyond the house was a barn which could be entered from the house or from outside. It consisted of a threshing floor lying between the cart and winnowing doors and mistals at the west end and on either side of the cart arch. There were a number of small outbuildings which would have housed hens and probably a pig or two.

This range of buildings has a complex history but seems to have originated in the early eighteenth century as a single-storey house with a thatched barn. By the end of the eighteenth century the house had two storeys and the barn had been raised and re-roofed in stone flags. During the nineteenth century the barn was extended to accommodate more cows and the house was raised a further 18 inches.

The land which was worked from this farmhouse consisted in 1851 of four acres of meadow and twelve acres of pasture with no arable land. Examination of earlier valuations of the farm shows that one field, Riding, a little over half an acre in extent, was almost certainly arable until 1838 or a little later. A number of the field names show that they had been intaken from the moor and the valuations reveal that this process was still continuing up to the mid-nineteenth century.

The whole farm was owned by the Taylors of Stanbury, who were the most prominent inhabitants of Stanbury village, being major landowners and trustees of Haworth church. It is not possible to say who were the first tenants but from at least 1811 the tenants were the Shackletons, who remained at Springs until the death of Benjamin Shackleton in 1878.

It is possible from the buildings and the records to build up a picture of the kind of farming practised at Springs. The mainstay of the farm would have been a small herd of dairy cattle, six at first which were pastured on the summering fields and over-wintered in the mistal using the hay from the mowing fields for feed. At this time half an acre of oats was grown in the field called Riding. The oats would have been mown with a sickle or scythe, dried in stooks in the field and hand threshed with flails in the barn. After threshing both barn doors would have been opened and a winnowing fan used to separate the chaff from the grain. The grain would have been taken to one of the local corn mills where it would be dried in a kiln before grinding to oatmeal. The oatmeal was used to make porridge and havercake – the staples of the local diet.

The necessity for growing their own grain must have declined, either owing to changes in the price of grain or improvements in transport links. Either way Ridings was converted to meadow by 1851 and more pasture was created by intaking from the moor. This intaking was heavy work; the rough moorland was dug over with mattock and spade and then limed. There are two likely sources for lime – the limestone quarries at Lothersdale six miles to the north and the glacial lime boulder workings at Boulsworth four miles to the west. From these sources lime was carried by packhorse trains heading into Calderdale and could no doubt readily be bought. After liming there may have been an initial root crop before the land was grassed. In these ways the pasture and meadow were extended to cater for the increased herd which was accommodated in extra mistals in the newly extended barn. The hay harvest was, of course, one of the main events in the farming year. The grass was mown with a scythe and dried in the fields before being taken to the barn by sled – or on a man's back using a hay rope. Here it was stored in the hay mow and fed to the cattle over the winter months.

The cows would have been kept mainly for milk from which butter and possibly cheese were made. Some beef may have been obtained from surplus bullocks. The presence of small outbuildings at Springs suggests that hens were kept to provide eggs and, occasionally, meat. In all probability a pig or two would also have been kept to add bacon to the diet.

It was common, as has been shown above, for a second trade to be followed by the tenants of these small moorland farms. The Shackletons of Springs worked as stone masons. There are numerous references in the census returns to various members of the family working as masons and in the 1840s Luke Shackleton & Sons appear as stone masons in the trade directories. It is not likely that they had their own quarry but there were a number of large stone quarries on the nearby Penistone Hill and they probably worked in one or other of these quarries.

It has been mentioned already that there was at one time a handloom at Springs. There is no indication that any of the Shackletons were involved in the textile trade but in the 1851 census a forty-eight-year-old handloom weaver, Abraham Sunderland, is entered at Springs. Comparison with other available records suggests that Sunderland was a sub-tenant of the Shackletons who supported himself by weaving stuff pieces.

After the death of the last of the Shackletons, Springs was tenanted by Luke Sunderland, who may have been related by marriage to the Shackletons. Sunderland continued to farm Springs and also worked as a stone mason. It is probable that he remained at Springs until the 1890s. A succession of tenants followed him but their occupations are not known to us. It is clear that the building of the Lower Laithe reservoir in the valley immediately below the farm would have had a profound effect. The water board was keen to stop farming and particularly the keeping of cows on water catchment areas; once a reservoir was built the farms around it tended to disappear. Although Springs was inhabited until the 1950s, it probably ceased to function as an independent farm after the completion of the reservoir in 1925. The land, along with that of a number of other farms on Enfieldside, is now given over to sheep grazing.

Springs remained empty for half a century until the rising value of rural housing persuaded the water board to sell off those farm buildings which were not too dilapidated and thus gave Springs a new lease of life.

two

Textiles

We do not know when cloth was first made in Haworth, but it would probably have been in medieval times. The first materials to be woven here would have been woollens which would have needed to be fulled. It is not known whether there was a fulling mill in Haworth or whether cloth had to be taken to the manorial mill in Bradford.

The weaving of worsteds was introduced into the Pennines around 1700 and we know that worsteds were being made in Haworth by the 1720s. This is proved by an entry in the parish registers which records the burial of a wool-comber in 1721. Wool combing was peculiar to the worsted trade, the wool for woollen fabrics being carded rather than combed. The marriage registers from 1754 to 1812 also record people's occupations and the vast majority are shalloon weavers – shalloon being a type of worsted cloth used for linings.

These early Haworth worsted weavers would have been working on handlooms in their own houses. The trade was organised and run by clothiers who would provide the weavers with yarn and would take the finished pieces to market. The combing and spinning of worsted yarns were also done by hand and finding enough yarn to keep the weavers employed was a constant struggle. It is known that manufacturers in the Haworth area were employing spinners far up into the Yorkshire Dales. The registers provide ample evidence that wool combing was being carried on in the area during the period from 1720 onwards but there is mention of only one spinner. This may well be because spinning was done by women and their occupations were largely ignored in the registers.

Spinning was the first of the textile processes to be mechanised and small mills started to appear in the third quarter of the eighteenth century. Midge Holme Mill at Leeming, one of the earliest spinning mills in the area, was built around 1790. The name of the nearby Throstle Nest Mill plays on the throstle on which the yarn was spun. Both these mills are now under Leeming reservoir.

Timothy Feather at his loom, *c.* 1900.

Whilst the spinning moved into the mills in the late eighteenth century, weaving continued to be done on handlooms in the weavers' cottages for many more decades. The 1841 census recorded fifty-four power-loom weavers and over a thousand other weavers – many of whom were probably also factory weavers. By the time of the 1851 census well over half of the 1,000 or so weavers were power-loom weavers. By 1861 less than 20% of the weavers were handloom weavers. The decline of the hand-weaving industry was clearly rapid, though a few older men continued to weave by hand for many years to come – the last dying in 1910. He was the well-known Timothy Feather of Buckley Green Bottom near Stanbury. 'Timmy' had lived in the same cottage all his life and had woven by hand for most of his life. In his later years he had become something of a tourist attraction and he was often photographed. As he himself said, 'Ya con buy me fer tuppence on a paast-card i' Stanbury or Haworth.' In many of these pictures he sits outside his cottage winding yarn onto bobbins for the shuttle – the bobbin winder which he uses is often mistaken for a spinning wheel but hand spinning had long since died out. It is often commented upon that Timmy wove cotton, not worsted cloth. This is true towards the end of his life but as he said, 'Aw used to weyve worsted an' aw cud addle summat then'. Timmy did once try weaving in a mill but 'Aw nivver made nowt o' paahr looms … aw liked mi own loom best at hooam, an' aw gav' ower in an hour or two.' Timmy's bedroom workshop with all his equipment can be seen at Cliffe Castle Museum in Keighley.

Wool combing was the last of the manufacturing processes to be mechanised but even this had moved into the factory by around 1860. Hand combing was a most unhealthy trade. The combs had to be used hot and this was achieved using a charcoal stove known as a pot. The wool to be combed had to be oiled and the combination of the heat, charcoal fumes and oil made for an unpleasant atmosphere. There is a local saying which recalls this atmosphere – 'It stinks war ner a kemming oil' (i.e. 'It smells worse than a comb shop'). In the great days of the hand trade, combers and handloom weavers could earn very respectable wages and could please themselves when they worked and when they 'laiked'. Stories are told of handloom weavers swaggering about with £5 notes stuck in their hat bands to indicate their affluence and independence. As the mechanisation of the trade gathered strength these hand workers were reduced to extreme poverty but the new discipline of the factory did not come easily to those used to this degree of freedom. The census figures show that the factory workers were a younger group than the hand workers and more of them were women.

The first spinning mills in Haworth Township appeared in the 1780s and 1790s and there were other early mills nearby at Addingham and Keighley. These first mills were relatively small affairs, were water powered and employed machines called throstles. The throstle was a modified form of Arkwright's water-frame and was named from the singing noise it made when working. At first many of these mills were spinning cotton yarns, the change to worsted yarn spinning occurring in the years around 1800.

A number of other spinning mills were also built to take advantage of the copious Pennine streams. These were often built in remote moorland places and it can come as a surprise to find mills marked on old maps at places like Bodkin and Forks House. The Forks House Mill is something of a mystery, having left virtually no trace on the ground and very little in the records. There are traces of a small mill goit and dam which documentary sources show to have been there by 1813. It is said to have been built around 1810 by Hiram Craven, whom we shall meet later. There is known to have been a comb shop at Forks and the presence of water power strongly suggests that this must have been a small spinning mill. The remains of the Forks farmhouse are seen by every visitor who walks up the Sladen Valley to Top Withins, but few will notice the nearby traces of this little mill.

Most of these early mills have vanished under reservoirs, been converted to housing or simply been demolished. Some idea of what such a mill might have looked like can be gained from a visit to Dunkirk Mill near Oxenhope. Here we have a virtually complete small mill complex. Beside the old road which leads from Hawksbridge to Leeshaw reservoir and then over to Hebden Bridge is the mill building and three attached cottages. Behind the main building is the now drained mill pond. Water from the pond ran into the mill and powered a small internal water-wheel. This wheel was later replaced by a water turbine. A delightful footpath follows the mill goit from the dam up the little valley of Leeshaw Water to a weir and the remains of a sluice gate. Here the water of the beck would have been diverted by the weir into the goit to feed the mill pond. A number of overflow channels can still be seen through which surplus water could be returned to the stream. The surviving mill building has a small chimney showing that water power was later supplemented, or replaced, by a steam engine.

Forks House with ruins of a comb shop in the foreground. The mill was a little way down to the right, *c.* 1950. [HH/KLS]

Dunkirk Mill, *c.* 1900. [KLS]

This mill was built by the Hartley family around 1800 as a worsted spinning mill but little remains of the original building. The mill was rebuilt in the 1880s, possibly by the Dewhirsts who had by then bought the mill from the Hartleys. It is largely this building which we see today. There was a later addition at the back and the engine house, boiler house and chimney were built on around 1900. These buildings now have a flat roof replacing the original pitched roof.

The different uses to which this little mill was put over the years reflect something of the vagaries of the textile industry. The Hartley family seem to have used it mostly for spinning worsted yarns. In the 1870s William Gawthorpe rented the mill from Hartley and was weaving cloth here. Dunkirk was empty for some time around 1880 but by 1886 it had passed into the ownership of the Dewhirst family (and subsequently their descendants the Heatons). They occupied the mill from then until 1972 when production ceased and their principal trade was making mill band. This was a kind of light cotton rope used to drive the spindles in spinning frames. Older readers from the northern mill towns will remember using a length of mill band to light fireworks on bonfire night. During the 1890s the Dewhirsts were using Dunkirk for wool combing, undoubtedly by machine and probably using the Noble comb. By 1901 the firm had returned to making cotton tapes for driving spindles and during the Second World War they wove webbing for the Forces. From about 1900 until at least 1936 there was also a corn dealer called Brooke (another relative of the Dewhirsts and Heatons) at Dunkirk, and it seems that the extension at the back of the main mill building was added for corn milling.

Another mill with early origins but a rather different history is Bridgehouse Mill in Haworth village. The early history of Bridgehouse is associated with the Greenwood family who were amongst the principal landowners in the area in the eighteenth and nineteenth centuries.

Bridgehouse Mill stands below Haworth village in the valley bottom where the turnpike road from Bradford crossed the Bridgehouse Beck. Since the construction of the railway the road adopts a slightly different line and no longer passes directly in front of the mill buildings.

The origins of Bridgehouse Mill seem to lie in an indigo mill which was mentioned in a Greenwood will of 1770. In this water-powered mill Greenwood ground and prepared the raw indigo from India for use in his dye house. The first spinning mill at Bridgehouse (later known as the Lower Mill) was built around 1781, making it the first such mill in Haworth Township. We know little about the water arrangements for this mill and this part of the valley was much altered when the railway was built in 1867. Before the construction of the railway there was a mill pond some distance upstream from Bridgehouse Mill but how it fed water to the Lower Mill is not obvious. It seems that this mill was first used for worsted spinning but was converted to cotton spinning in 1784. There was another experiment in worsted spinning at Bridgehouse in the late 1780s but it soon reverted to cotton spinning in which trade it continued until around 1810.

Some time around 1810 a second mill (the Upper Mill) was built by James Greenwood and the firm began to spin worsted, rather than cotton, yarns again. At this time Greenwood also constructed the long goit which still exists to bring water to the wheel at the new mill. The Bridgehouse goit starts at a sluice gate a good half mile upstream from the mill. There is no mill

Bridgehouse Mills – an idealised view from an early twentieth-century advertising card. The four-storey buildings are for spinning, the weaving sheds are single storey. Note the presence of both water-wheel and steam power. [KLS]

pond in connection with the upper mill but the goit itself widens considerably towards the mill and would have provided some storage capacity. It is from this goit that the mill pond mentioned above was fed, the pond possibly having been built at this time. As was indicated above, it is not clear what became of the water from this pond; no outlet is apparent on the maps other than one letting water back into the stream.

In 1832 James Greenwood junior built himself a fine new mansion some distance from the mill at Woodlands. An earlier mill owner's house, Bridgehouse, which survives next to the mill buildings, dates in its present form from 1746.

Also around the 1830s a steam engine was erected at the mill to supplement the water-wheel. The last surviving wheel at Bridgehouse was about 60 feet in diameter, 9 feet wide and developed 100 horse power.

We can get some picture of working conditions at Bridgehouse in 1834 from the Greenwoods' answers to a Factory Commission questionnaire. The mill is said to have been built around 1791 (although, as we have seen, it was rather earlier) and to spin worsted yarns by water power. There were sixty employees (exclusive of clerical and warehouse staff) most of them between the ages of ten and eighteen. These children earned from 3 to 5 shillings a week, the girls earning a slightly higher rate than the boys. This changes markedly once the workers reach the age of twenty-one when men were paid 18s a week and women only 7s 6d. The working week was six days from 6 a.m. to 8 p.m. with an hour for dinner. Other meals were brought in by parents and friends and were taken without stopping the machinery. In times of drought the mill often had to stop work during the day and could not re-start for two or three hours. Sometimes the Greenwoods bore the cost, at other times the workers had to make up the lost time. Eight whole

Water-wheel at Bridgehouse Mills, *c.* 1900. The trough delivering water to the wheel is clearly visible. Note the weaving shed to the left and spinning mill behind the wheel.

days and three half days were the holiday allowance, unpaid unless the hours were made up. Finally the Greenwoods aver that no corporal punishment of the children is sanctioned. Proof that not all those who have been involved in running Bridgehouse were so compassionate came to light a few years ago when a mill master's cane was found behind a cupboard.

In 1848 the Greenwoods' business failed and their Haworth estate was sold. The mill and Woodlands House were acquired by Richard Shackleton Butterfield who considerably enlarged the mill and started weaving as well as spinning at Bridgehouse.

There is a good deal of confusion about the precise history of the surviving buildings and their relationship to those mentioned in the records. The house next to the mill buildings is Georgian in style and is the result of an extension, or rebuilding of an earlier house carried out by the Greenwoods in 1746. The Upper Mill stood at the end of the goit and has gone completely. The older of the two mill buildings visible from the road looks to belong to the period around 1800 with its characteristic stepped window on the first floor and a Venetian window on the second floor (which was lost to fire in 2001). There is also a splendid mask keystone in the cart arch. The various plans of the mill make it clear that this building must, in fact, date from after 1850, which is rather puzzling; one wonders if this was deliberate archaism or whether some elements of an earlier building are incorporated.

Of the Lower Spinning Mill and indigo mill nothing survives and the part of the site nearest the beck is now occupied by a large spinning mill built by Butterfield after the construction of the nearby railway line had diverted the stream. The weaving sheds, of various dates after 1850, lie behind this building.

In contrast to the small spinning mill at Dunkirk which underwent very limited expansion, Bridgehouse Mill grew from its small beginnings to be a moderately large spinning and weaving mill. In common with Dunkirk however it suffered from the decline in the textile industry in the twentieth century and has been put to a variety of uses. It continued to house a variety of worsted spinning and weaving firms until 1974 and since then has been used for more varied purposes. These have included biscuit making, chicken processing, spring making and the sale of antiques and exotic birds. One of the principal firms still in the building is the last remaining textile producer in Haworth, making narrow fabrics for military and ceremonial use. Amongst their more unusual products are false eyelashes for camels!

Dunkirk and Bridgehouse are only two of some thirty mills which have worked in Haworth Township but their stories might be taken as representative of the smaller and larger concerns respectively. Many of the old mills have vanished without trace or been converted to housing. Two which survive, one in ruins, deserve attention. In the Worth Valley below Stanbury lie the picturesque remains of Griffe Mill. Griffe started as a cotton-spinning mill in the 1790s, converted to worsted spinning around 1820 and expanded in the middle of the nineteenth century to include weaving sheds as well as a six-storey spinning mill. The remains of the mill are ruinous but extensive. The goit can be traced from a sharp bend in the river some distance upstream to the now drained mill pond immediately above the buildings. The wheel pit is still to be found and there are the remains of a large pipe running into the top of the pit. This was used to feed water to a turbine which replaced the water-wheel. A mill chimney also survives indicating that the water power was, here as in many other local mills, supplemented by steam power in the nineteenth century. Large parts of the spinning mill survive as do the remains of a dwelling where, in 1841 the mill manager Stephen Merrall lived. By 1848 the mill had passed into the hands of John Williamson and the house was inhabited by the mill overlooker in 1851 and 1861. Williamsons continued to spin and weave worsted here until the turn of the century when Griffe was acquired by William Wallbank who returned it to cotton spinning until at least 1922.

One interesting feature to be seen at Griffe, just beyond the little bridge over the Worth, is a circular grassy mound with a deep hollow in the middle. This was the site of the mill's gas holder. Many textile mills, particularly in rural locations, made their own gas for lighting. This was necessary when hours of daylight were short in winter and the hours of work were long. The primitive gas jets which lit these mills would have been a great improvement on tallow candles and probably cheaper as well.

The most complete surviving textile mill in Haworth is Ebor Mill which stands beside the Bridgehouse Beck at the northern end of the township. The first mill was erected here by Hiram Craven of Oakworth around 1819. This building survives alongside Ebor Lane. Although it is now converted into offices, the arch through which water flowed to the wheel is still visible. Behind this original mill there is a large cobbled yard with the later mill buildings set around it. These include engine, boiler and economiser houses, a magnificent chimney, weaving sheds, warehouses and, most obviously, a fine six-storey spinning mill of 1887. Whilst a few mills in the area still house some form of industry, these fine old buildings are increasingly being converted for housing. Usually one or two of the more impressive buildings are converted into apartments, the remainder being demolished and houses built on the site. This fate may well await the important mill complex at Ebor.

three

Stone and Coal

The third main industry in the Haworth area after farming and textiles was stone quarrying. The moors around the township are scarred with dozens of old quarries, most of them quite small.

The stone which has been worked in this area was all deposited around 315 million years ago in the vast delta of a river which ran from ancient mountains to the north. The rocks laid down at this time are collectively known as the Millstone Grit. They consist of a thick series of gritstones, sandstones and shales with the occasional thin coal seam. These different types of rock reflect the changing sea levels at the time they were deposited – the fine-grained shales in deeper water, the sandstones and grits in the shallower water of the delta whereas coal formed from the vegetation of swamps.

The stones which occur in the Haworth area are amongst the youngest of the Millstone Grit rocks. Three main groups have been quarried in the area: the Rough Rock and Rough Rock Flags, the Woodhouse Grit and the Kinderscout Grits. The shales between the sandstones are generally of little interest to the quarryman but a new use which has been found for them will be mentioned later.

The youngest of these stones is the Rough Rock which caps the highest hills around Haworth. It is a tough, coarse-grained rock which is impervious to water. The Rough Rock was used for building stone and for heavy jobs such as dock gates, bridge foundations, engine beds and warehouse basements. It was quarried on Black Moor and at Delf Hill at the north end of Nab Hill.

Under the Rough Rock comes a series of flagstones which, according to thickness, can be used for roofing slates, paving stones or for building. These Rough Rock Flags were quarried at the Woodcock, Fly, Nab Hill and Deep Arse delfs on Nab Hill and at Cuckoo Park on Black Moor.

The next workable rock below the Rough Rock Flags is known as the Woodhouse Grit. This was the most important rock in the area and provided both flagstones of various thicknesses and

Flappit Spring Quarry, *c.* 1890. A busy scene in a quarry on Black Moor. [ID]

blocks of good-quality building stone. The main areas in which this stone was quarried were at Crow Hill near the Lancashire border, at Naylor Hill Quarry on Brow Moor and at the West End, Fieldhead and Penistone Quarries on Penistone Hill.

The oldest stone worked locally is the Kinderscout Grit which is variable in texture and quality. The coarser grades were used for grindstones and gave the Millstone Grit its name. There is a small, disused quarry near the road to Hebden Bridge called Grinding Stone Hole where these were obtained. The Kinderscout Grits were also quarried for building stone, walling and pitching (that is rough paving with small slabs). There was a small quarry at Dyke Nook – also near the Hebden Bridge road, but the largest quarries for this stone were at Bankfield Quarry near Haworth village and at Dimples Quarry on Penistone Hill.

Finally there is a very hard, fine-grained rock known as Keighley Bluestone which was prized as a source of road metal. The main quarries for this were on the north side of the Worth Valley at Hare Hill Edge but Bluestone was quarried (and mined) in Haworth Township on Bracken Hill Edge near Ponden Clough.

Stone would have been quarried in early times for building and for field walls. Demand would have risen in response to a number of developments: the increase in stone building from about 1600, the making of canals, turnpike roads and the enclosing of the commons in the eighteenth century; the building of mills and of houses for the mill workers from around 1800. The growth of nearby towns such as Keighley and Bradford would also have greatly expanded the demand for building and paving stone. In the Haworth district a further impetus to the production of stone would have come with the building of the reservoirs and the railway in the 1860s and '70s. In the later twentieth century much stone has been quarried to be crushed for aggregate or sand.

The early quarries would have been very small ones dug to build only one or two houses or to wall a few fields. Such quarries are liberally scattered over the moors of the upper Worth Valley. Larger, commercial quarries came with the Industrial Revolution. There is evidence of great growth in the local quarrying industry in the mid-nineteenth century.

There are three particularly significant areas of quarrying in Haworth Township: Black Moor, Penistone Hill and Nab Hill. Each of these will now be considered in rather more detail.

Brow Moor and Black Moor form a strip of high land at the eastern end of Haworth Township and have one working and numerous disused quarries. The disused quarries on the Black Moor itself worked the youngest rock of the Millstone Grit, the Rough Rock. As is noted above this is a tough rock which is unaffected by water. It was used as a building stone and particularly for engine beds. These were massive blocks of stone which could be ten tons in weight and were used to provide a stable foundation for the steam engines which powered Yorkshire's textile mills.

To the north of the Black Moor, on the edge of Brow Moor, is Naylor Hill Quarry which is still the most active working quarry in the area. Naylor Hill was already a significant quarry by 1850 but has since extended very considerably. The earliest quarry owner of whom we have any record is James Booth, who had Naylor Hill from at least 1889 to 1912. Booth was followed by Greenwood & Co. in the 1920s and since the 1940s Naylor Hill has been run by Dennis Gillson & Co. Dennis Gillson at first rented the quarry from the Craven Water Board and later bought it from Yorkshire Water. The stone produced here is from the upper part of the Woodhouse Grit and finds many uses. As Dennis Gillson himself said in 1975, 'We can produce anything in the building trade … it is good stone.' The shale overburden of the grit has also been worked here to make impervious linings for local landfill sites.

Penistone Hill was the main quarrying area of Haworth hamlet and had four large quarries working two different ages of rock. Just above Haworth village, and now forming its main tourist car park, was Bankfield Quarry in the Kinderscout Grits. It first appeared on the map as a small quarry around 1890 and gradually expanded up until the 1930s. Bankfield was run by Alexander Dyson in the 1890s and 1900s and then by Charlie Gillson. In the 1920s it passed into the hands of Jagger Bros with whose name it is most associated. It has the reputation of having been a hard place to work and it is still sometimes referred to locally as Heartbreak Hill. The quarry owner used to say that he liked to see a man walking up the path to work whistling in the morning and going home at night holding the handrail. It continued to work until 1970 but was then converted into a car park. One of the quarry buildings found a new use around 1980 when it was employed as the Haworth Brass Band's practise room.

Higher on the hill is the quarry at Dimples which also worked the Kinderscout Grits. It was already in use by 1850 and was extended southwards over the ensuing decades. There appear

Naylor Hill Quarry, 2004. A general view of Gillson's quarry. [SCW]

Naylor Hill Quarry, 2004. Some of the machinery of a modern quarry. [SCW]

to have been three firms operating at Dimples from around 1890 or 1900 – Andrews & Co., Sladden, Shackleton & Co. and Pedley, Metcalfe & Co. The latter company continued to operate at Dimples until at least 1927. Dimples was one of the two principal quarries supplying stone for the construction of Lower Laithe reservoir which was built in the valley below the quarry between 1912 and 1925. The course of the railway line from the quarry to the embankment area is now a much-used track between Haworth and Stanbury. This quarry was later run by Jagger Bros and finally closed around 1970.

The other two quarries on Penistone Hill both exploited the Woodhouse Grits and so will have produced a variety of building, paving and roofing stones. The first of these was Penistone Quarry itself which had already achieved almost its full extent by 1850 when it had an annual rental value estimated at £80 – more than four times as much as any other quarry in the township. It was then operated by Thomas & George Hilliary. From around 1880 to 1910 it was run by John & Jonas Sutcliffe. It finally ceased to work around 1939 – the first of the Penistone Hill quarries to close. Large holes in the ground are very attractive to those with rubbish to dispose of and Penistone Quarry was being used as a rubbish tip by the 1960s.

Finally we have the West End Quarry near the cricket ground on the moor edge above Higher Marsh. West End is already to be seen on the map of 1847 but grew considerably over the years. By 1896 it had a rateable value of £40; all the other quarries on Penistone Hill had values of around £15 each. It is particularly associated with the firm of Charles Barrett & Co. who ran it from around 1875 until 1942. Charles Barrett was succeeded by his son Kershaw Barrett who, when not running his quarries, made fine violins in his workshop at the old grammar school in Marsh. The Barretts were the most important quarrying family in the area, producing large block stone at West End which was sold on to be cut up into ashlar building stone – from which much of Bradford is built. They also worked the nearby Fieldhead Quarry for flagstone. West End was briefly reopened around 1967-69 by the Mace brothers.

There is much of geological interest to be seen on Penistone Hill. A fine section in the Kinderscout Grits is exposed at Dimples Quarry which demonstrates the cyclical deposition of sandstones and shales in varying environments in the Carboniferous delta. There is a thin 'smudge' of coal with its associated seat earth in this section as well as a large fossil stigmarian root. Cliffe Castle Museum in Keighley has an interpretation of this section in its excellent geology department. At West End Quarry there is a good section of the Woodhouse Grit which clearly shows the current bedding which developed in the delta. A large cavity in this section represents what the quarry men called a 'mare' – an area of soft stone which is rapidly weathered away. It was useless for building stone but was ground up and mixed with cement to make 'donkey stones' for scouring doorsteps.

Some years ago a heritage trail was established on Penistone Hill to explain its quarrying industry to the interested visitor. The markers for this trail are still in place and there is a newly revised edition of the leaflet which should be obtainable from the Tourist Information Centre in Haworth.

High above the Oxenhope Valley stands Nab Hill, which reaches a height of almost 1,500 feet above sea level. The top of the hill is formed of Rough Rock which was quarried at Delf

West End Quarry, *c.* 1910. Bob Barrett stands at the quarry face. [RM]

West End Quarry, *c.* 1910. Steam cranes work at the quarry top. [RM]

Hill, probably for the construction of the Thornton Moor reservoir in the 1870s. Most of the quarries on Nab Hill worked the underlying Rough Rock Flags for various grades of building stone, paving flags and roof 'slates' or thackstones.

The principal quarries were Deep House Delf, Nab Hill, Woodcock and, just outside Haworth Township, Fly Delf. Deep House is a misnomer introduced by the Ordnance Survey which clearly did not like the local name, Deep Arse. When I first walked amongst the Nab Hill quarries thirty years ago it was a remarkable landscape of deep sunken roads linking the quarry workings. One walked along the narrow, winding roads between stone retaining walls well below the level of the moor. Unfortunately nearly all of these tracks have been lost as quarrying work has sporadically continued at Nab Hill.

A very interesting aspect of the Nab Hill stone industry is that some beds of stone were mined rather than being worked in open quarries. There were a number of shallow shafts sunk to the level of the bed to be worked. From the foot of these shafts there would have been drifts extending outwards from which the flags were extracted. We have a good account of similar mines in the Elland Flags of the Brighouse district (Godwin, C.G., *Mining in the Elland Flags*, London, HMSO, 1984).

Godwin describes how the shafts were sunk by hand to the required depth and a couple of feet of overburden was then removed from the top of the bed to be worked. Once this free space had been created leaves of rock could be removed by driving wedges into a bedding plane thus lifting a leaf of rock into the void above. The rock was carried to the shaft bottom using a yoke and wound up the shaft with a windlass or gin. These mines in the Elland Flags sometimes reached a depth of 150 feet and were, after about 1860, wound by steam power. The Nab Hill mines were almost certainly on a smaller scale – the shafts, when open thirty years ago, were found to be only about 10 or 15 feet in depth. A couple of the collapsed shafts can still be found on Nab Hill but may be lost as quarrying continues.

Stone was also mined in two other locations in Haworth. The Woodhouse Grits were mined in an adit at the Crow Hill Quarries high on Stanbury Moor. Roofing slates from Crow Hill were sent as far afield as Liverpool. Secondly there was an adit on Bracken Hill Edge near Ponden Clough. In this mine, and in a series of small quarries, Keighley Bluestone was dug for use as road metal.

The principal names associated with the Nab Hill quarries were: Standworths at Deep House and Fly in the 1860s and '70s, Bancroft at Deep House from 1877 to 1897 (and quite possibly to 1936 or later), Pickles at Deep House and Fly from 1877 to 1904 and Dawson at Woodcock from 1860 to 1880. Activities were restarted at Fly by R. Mace & Sons in 1971 and a number of firms have worked the Nab Hill quarries since then. The only old plan of quarry workings which I have been able to find shows the Woodcock Hall Quarries in 1854.

Turning to the people who worked in the stone trade, the mid-century census returns for Haworth Township give us an insight into who was actually doing the work in the quarries. They do not tell us which quarry a man worked in but it is possible to distinguish two groups according to where they lived: those most likely to be working on Penistone Hill and those probably employed at Black Moor or Nab Hill.

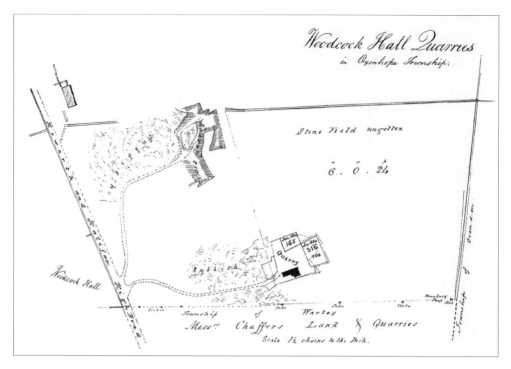

Plan of Woodcock Hall Quarry, 1854. [WYAS, Bfd]

In 1841 there were thirty-four boys and men employed in the stone industry, roughly half of them on Penistone and half in the Black Moor/Nab Hill area with one or two working on Stanbury Moor. Again they are split about evenly between those employed in quarrying stone and stone masons working the stone. Two thirds of these workers were thirty or under and three of them were boys. None was over the age of sixty-five.

By 1851 the figure had risen to around 100 with thirty being masons. The ages were rather higher with half the men being over the age of thirty. Around sixty of the men were working on Penistone, most of the rest being in the Oxenhope quarries and half a dozen or so on Stanbury Moor.

The figures are very similar in 1861 although the proportion working on Penistone Hill had declined from half to a third. The Haworth census returns do not give a full picture of the numbers working on Nab Hill – many of the workers will have lived in the Denholme and Ogden areas. There are said to have been fifteen firms working on Nab Hill in the 1860s. They employed upwards of 300 men, and fifty or more horses were required to haul away the stone. One notable feature in the 1861 census is that a number of workers are specifically stated to be flag and slate quarriers. They were to be found both at Nab Hill and near Ponden. This is good evidence for the quarrying (or mining) of roof 'slates' in both the Woodhouse Grits and the Rough Rock Flags.

Haworth's other extractive industry was coal mining. It is perhaps surprising to find that coal was mined in the Haworth area, which lies almost entirely on the Millstone Grit. However there are a number of thin beds of coal at various horizons in the Millstone Grit and some of these were worked in the Haworth area. It must also be noted that the Yorkshire coal field just reaches into the south-east corner of Haworth Township. Thus we have three areas in which coal was mined: Sawood and Cobling in the Coal Measures proper; Penistone Hill and Stanbury Moor both in the Millstone Grit.

All the mine shafts are now either collapsed or capped and little remains to be seen of this industry. There are a few small adits (mostly for drainage) to be seen in the Sladen Valley. It was probably one of these that Joseph Craven (*Stanbury : A Brontë Moorland Village*, Keighley, 1907) entered to visit a friend: 'I once went up this mine in a trolley to see one of my companions. We had nothing but a candle with us, and when we reached my friend he was lying on his side working at the seam – a very shallow one.' A brief but telling description of a local coal mine. Craven also tells us that a man called Clayton was lost in one of the Stanbury coal mines and was never found. There was the short-lived Stanbury Coal, Iron & Lead Mining Co. in the 1860s but it does not seem to have been very successful.

There is no mention of coal mines in nineteenth-century trade directories but the firm of Richard Ayrton & Co. features in records of the 1850s. They were operating a coal pit at Cobling near Sawood. Little apart from a large retaining wall survives at Cobling but there are a number of shallower bell pits to be seen in the surrounding area. The 1841 census returns show that there were eighteen coal miners working in the Sawood area. The youngest was eight; half were fifteen or under. The numbers of miners at Sawood remained constant from 1841 to 1861. By 1871 the number dropped to no more than eight and probably only four. This rapid decline almost certainly reflects the arrival of the railway at Oxenhope in 1867. This would bring in cheaper, better-quality coal from the main mining areas of the Yorkshire coalfield and effectively end local mining operations.

The census returns seem to show that there were a dozen or so miners working on Penistone Hill in 1841 and none thereafter. In 1861 there were around ten miners in the Stanbury district. These figures may indicate that the Penistone Hill coal seams were worked out by 1850 and that mining activity shifted to Stanbury Moor, but this is uncertain.

There is an interesting entry in the 1841 census returns for Hill Top near Penistone Hill. Two brothers aged ten and eight are described as a gin horse driver and a chisel carrier. The younger boy was probably working in the quarries taking tools to the smithy to be sharpened and returning them to the men in the quarry. There is an upright stone near West End Quarry which formed part of the smithy hearth. The elder brother was employed leading the horse which worked a gin or hoist – this might have been to lift stone from a quarry or it might have wound a coal mine shaft. There is said to be a gin track visible from the air near the Forth Ponds on Penistone Hill.

four

Road and Rail

The industries described in the first three chapters were all to some extent dependent on roads. Farms used tracks and footpaths between their fields and their outlying moorland pastures and peat diggings. Quarries and coal mines required well constructed, easily graded roads to get their heavy produce to its destination. The textile industry was dependent upon a complex network of packhorse tracks connecting the clothiers with their sources of raw material, their home workers and their markets. Up to the eighteenth century roads were largely a local affair and were maintained, or more often neglected, by the parish. Routes were often general and indistinct, following trends rather than lines. As one part of a route became unusable due to rutting and mud, a different line was taken until that in its turn became equally unusable. In this way the road drifted from side to side across a broad swathe of land. The eighteenth century saw the introduction of turnpike roads which were maintained by trustees and for the use of which toll charges were levied.

The first road of more than local significance to pass through Haworth Township was the medieval Clitheroegate which connected two great estates of the De Lacy family – the Honour of Pontefract and the Honour of Clitheroe. This ancient road, which is first mentioned in a deed of 1240, came from Bradford to Haworth over Brow Moor and passed westwards through Stanbury to Ponden and Colne. It is thought that the De Lacys had an important staging post on this route in the neighbourhood of Stanbury. This was probably at Old Snap where there is known to have been a settlement from at least the fourteenth century.

The main traces left by the packhorse tracks are their bridges and some stretches of holloway – deeply entrenched paths lying well below the surrounding ground level. The paved packhorse ways, locally known as causeys, are much less evident in the Haworth area than in upper Calderdale. Occasional stretches of causey are to be met with but they often have the look of footways across the fields for the use of mill workers.

Long Bridge, *c.* 1900. The packhorse track is seen approaching the bridge on the right-hand side of the stream. [KLS]

The network of packhorse tracks across Haworth Township is complex and difficult to disentangle from other kinds of route. The only points where we can be certain of the route of a packhorse way are the bridges, causeys and holloways. One route crosses the township from north-west to south-east, is reasonably clear and offers examples of all these features. It has no name overall but starts as Street Lane on the north side of the Worth near Oldfield. This name is interesting and might possibly indicate a Roman road. Street Lane descends the valley side obliquely towards Long Bridge. When it reaches Lumb Foot Beck a branch drops steeply down to Lumb Foot Bridge. This branch is the best example of a causey in the area. The main route continues the line of Street Lane but is now called Hey Lane. In this section much of the route is a holloway. Hey Lane reaches the River Worth at its confluence with Sladen Beck and crosses it by Long Bridge, a very fine example of a packhorse bridge. The route climbs steeply out of the valley by way of another holloway known as Oldfield Gate. This is probably the finest section of holloway in the township although it is much overgrown and the revetment wall has been destroyed for the sake of its stone in recent years. Above Oldfield Farm the track crosses the Blue Bell turnpike and strikes out across Penistone Hill. At the southern end of Penistone Hill several different routes are available. One of these was either by way of Higher Marsh or by Hole Farm to Old Oxenhope. Here the route turns north towards Haworth for a short distance until an obvious packhorse way is picked up at Marsh End. Here a narrow, walled holloway, Cow Rake, drops down to the Bridgehouse Beck which it crosses by another very fine packhorse bridge, North Ives Bridge. This bridge is always known locally as the Donkey Bridge. The track then climbs diagonally up the valley side to cross the Hebden Bridge Turnpike at Royd House. Above the turnpike road the way winds up the hillside to Delf Hill and Black Moor Road. From here to the township boundary the route is a very wide, walled road called Cuckoo Park Lane. The width of this road betrays its origin as an enclosure road set out in the Oxenhope Enclosure Act of 1771 to take the packhorse track through the newly enclosed lands to the unenclosed moorland beyond. From here the route crosses the Black Moor towards Cullingworth and Denholme. Beyond these villages routes would have continued to Bradford and Halifax.

To the west of this route is another along which the 'lime gals' (Galloway ponies) brought lime from Craven or from Lancashire for use on the acid soils of Airedale and Calderdale. On a map of 1847 a section of this Limersgate is delineated between South Dean near Stanbury and the township boundary on Oxenhope Edge. Nowhere is it very obvious on the ground.

The valleys and, particularly, the moorlands of the Haworth area offer numerous examples of other types of early road. The enclosure roads created under the Oxenhope enclosure of the 1770s have already been mentioned. The remarkable vanished quarry roads of Nab Hill were noted in the previous chapter. The Nab Hill area, despite these losses, remains a very good place to study the roads associated with the stone industry.

Turbary roads, by which peat was brought from the peat diggings on the moors to heat the area's houses, are still to be seen. A very striking example lies on Withins Height near the Alcomden Stones. Clearly visible in aerial photographs is a long, perfectly straight line on the moor. Examined at close quarters it proves to be a sunken track over 6 feet in depth and some 200 yards long. The 1847 6-inch map shows that it formed part of a track which ran from the farms of the Sladen Valley and Ponden areas to the moor near the Alcomden Stones where it simply stopped just short of the township boundary. It was clearly built with great effort, yet it does not go anywhere and there is no quarry at its end. The sole remaining explanation for it is that it was a turbary road. One used to have to trespass to visit the Alcomden Stones (which, incidentally, are not any kind of prehistoric monument as is often claimed but a good example of a scarp edge tor) and the turbary road, but 'Right to Roam' legislation has now made this fascinating area freely accessible.

The largely local network of roads with makeshift arrangements for their maintenance continued to serve Haworth until the mid-eighteenth century. It was in 1755 that an Act was passed for a turnpike road from Bradford to Colne. The road became known as the Blue Bell turnpike from the name of its terminus near Colne.

The Act allowed for the 'amending' of an already existing road – the ancient Clitheroegate – rather than the construction of a new road. This involved the filling in of ruts and hollows, the levelling of humps, widening of the road in places and the widening or rebuilding of bridges. The maximum extent of changes in both the level and width of the road was about 5 feet.

Above: The turbary road on Withins Height. The line of the road is clearly indicated by the members of the Ramblers' Association celebrating the first day of open access, 19 September 2004. [SCW]

Right: Act of Parliament authorising the Blue Bell Turnpike, 1755.

Anno vicesimo octavo

Georgii II. Regis.

An Act for amending and widening the Roads from the West End of *Toller Lane* near *Bradford*, through *Haworth* in the County of *York*, to a Place called *Blue Bell*, near *Colne* in the County of *Lancaster*; and from a Place called *The Two Laws*, to *Kighley* in the said County of *York*.

WHEREAS the Road lead-ing from the West End of Toller Lane near Bradford, over Chelley Height and Cullingworth Moor, through Haworth and Standbury, to a Place called The Two Laws in the County of York, and so by Lanshaw Bridge, to a Place called Blue Bell, near the Town of Colne in the County Palatine of Lancaster; and the Road branching from the said Place called The Two Laws, to Kighley in the said County of York, where the Road from Bradford and Kighley to the said Town of Colne unite, are in a very ruinous Condition, and in some Places not

8 R 2   only

The road was also to be covered with small stone to a depth of up to 12 inches. Only one diversion of the route was made and that was near the Herders' Inn over the Lancashire border. The initial improvements were made in the first two years at a cost of £1,250. Of the first £1,000 subscribed just over half came from three Haworth investors, Joseph Midgley the Lord of the Manor, John Greenwood of Bridgehouse Mill and William Grimshaw the perpetual curate.

The route of the turnpike road through Haworth Township was a veritable switchback. The road entered Haworth at the top of Brow Moor and dropped over 300 feet to Bridgehouse. There is an oddity as the road makes its final approach to Bridgehouse when it abandons a gradual line of descent to plunge steeply down the final 150 yards to Bridgehouse – this presumably reflects a choice made in medieval times, the reasons for which are lost. From the bridge at Bridgehouse the road climbs up through Haworth village for 200 feet to West Lane. Here the descent of Hollings Brow to Sladen Bridge commences. At the foot of this steep descent is a stone built into the wall bearing the legend 'Hang on'. This was discovered by workmen in 1997 and caused much puzzlement at the time. An entry in the minute book for 1764 may hold the answer. This allows carts to be drawn up Hollings Brow by specified numbers of horses depending on the size of the cart. I believe that 'Hang on' was an instruction to carters to stop at Sladen Bridge and take on extra horses for the climb up to Haworth village. From Sladen Bridge the road climbs again to Stanbury, passes though the village and drops gradually to Ponden Bridge. Here begins the final climb to Two Laws, the Lancashire boundary and Combe Hill where the road reaches its summit at 1,150 feet above sea level.

As it crosses Haworth Township the turnpike makes use of three bridges – at Bridgehouse, Sladen and Ponden. Bridgehouse Bridge was to be widened by 2 yards and have its walls raised; this was to cost £15. Ponden and Sladen becks were to have new bridges built at a cost of £37 10s and £20 respectively. All of these bridges have been either replaced or substantially rebuilt since they were made for the turnpike. The old bridge at Bridgehouse was replaced by the present one, on a different line of road, when the railway was built in the 1860s. Sladen and Ponden bridges were strengthened in the 1990s.

The toll houses were situated at Brow Top (although this may have been for the Hebden Bridge Road), the bottom of Main Street, near the Sun Inn on West Lane and at the west end of Stanbury village. Here travellers would be required to make payments to use the road. The tolls, as set in 1803, included 1s 3d per score of cattle; 8d a score for calves, sheep or swine; 1d for a horse and charges of up to 3s for wheeled vehicles depending on the type of vehicle and the number of horses drawing it. For the first six years the tolls were collected by Rowland Watson who was the Manor Steward. From 1761 the tolls were let out annually. The auctions were held in public houses and were lively affairs. J.J. Brigg in his account of the Keighley & Kendal Trust records the story of a man 'thrown from a gig and killed driving home from a toll-letting'. Amongst those who took the Blue Bell tolls were a number of Haworth men including Joseph Pighells, clothier, of Intack around 1800 and Robert Wright, clogger, of Haworth around 1815. The minutes of the Blue Bell Trust end in 1823 but there are miscellaneous records up to 1860. The toll house and gates at the bottom of Main Street were bought by the Haworth Local Board in 1860. The toll house was demolished to allow for the widening of the road.

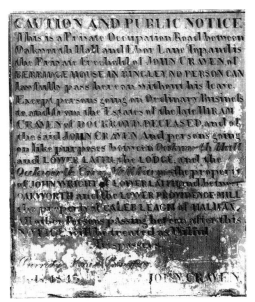

Above left: The 'Hang on' stone at Sladen Bridge. [SCW]

Above right: Private road notice at Ebor Lane.[SCW]

The other turnpike road in the township was a very different affair. The Lees & Hebden Bridge Road was much later, being built under an Act of 1813, and was a completely new road. It is the road which starts at Lees near Cross Roads and runs high along the east side of the valley of the Bridgehouse Beck to Oxenhope and thence over Cock Hill Moor to Hebden Bridge – today's A6033. The road was built by Hiram Craven of Dockroyd near Oakworth, a notable local contractor. He has already been mentioned as the builder of the little mill at Forks House around 1810. That was said to have been his first contract, if so he had come a long way by the time he undertook the construction of over eight miles of turnpike road climbing 1,000 feet over the exposed moors between Airedale and Calderdale.

Craven (or one his sons) was responsible for another toll road in Haworth but this one was not a turnpike but a private road. Ebor and Providence Lanes served the mills which Craven owned, Ebor in Haworth and Providence in Oakworth. They run from Mill Hey in Haworth to Oakworth Hall and there are stone plaques at each end and at a toll house at the junction of the two lanes at Mytholmes. These are dated 1843 and set out, at considerable length, the conditions under which the road may be used. Tolls were charged for the use of this road until it was taken over by the Local Authority in 1934. The toll-gate posts were pulled out by Haworth council's steam roller, having proved too big a job for horses. Hiram Craven's most famous creation is the Ouse Bridge at York – he succeeded in bridging the river where many had failed before him. He was made a freeman of the city in recognition of his achievement. These connections adequately explain the names of Ebor Mill and Ebor Lane in Haworth which were made about the same time as his Ouse Bridge (Eboracum being the Roman name for York). Craven's name is remembered to this day in Oxenhope. His Hebden Bridge Road enters the village crossing over Leeming Water by a bridge still known as Hiram Brig.

One other turnpike road is relevant to the Haworth area: the Keighley & Halifax Trust. This was formed in 1753 but it was not until 1794 that a new road from Keighley to Cross Roads was constructed. Its approach to Cross Roads is still called New Road Side. This road does not enter Haworth Township but will obviously have effected a radical improvement in Haworth's connection to Keighley. The road which connects the Halifax turnpike to Haworth was known as Sikes Lane. It is described as a turnpike road on an estate map of 1848 but does not seem to be covered by any Act. Perhaps it started to be maintained to turnpike standards when the 1794 road was built. The same map also describes the Haworth to Oxenhope road along Sun Street as a turnpike, which it was not.

After the construction of the Hebden Bridge turnpike around 1814 there was no great improvement in road communications until the advent of the motor car forced major changes around 1930.

Keighley had a rail connection to Bradford and Leeds by 1847. Haworth's mills and other industries continued to be hampered by poor communications for a further twenty years. The lack of a railway made the importation of raw materials and fuel (particularly coal) and the exportation of merchandise very expensive. A number of railway schemes were proposed but nothing came of them until the local mill owners decided to act for themselves.

A meeting was held at the Black Bull Inn in 1861, possibly at the initial suggestion of the engineer John McLandsborough, to explore the possibility of providing Haworth with a railway. Over the following year there was much argument as to the precise route to be taken. The Worth Valley mill owners were the principal investors and each, of course, wanted the railway to come close to his mill. Eventually the route to Haworth and then up the Bridgehouse Beck Valley to Lowertown was agreed upon – the Oxenhope mill owners having to find the extra money for the section beyond Haworth. It would have seemed more sensible to extend the railway to the far end of Oxenhope village where a number of mills stood. This, however, would have advantaged these mills over those of another of the investors and so was not to be contemplated. Instead the railway company built Station Road to connect the mills to the goods yard.

Money and agreement as to route secured, the directors obtained their Act of Parliament for the line in 1862 and, with John McLandsborough as engineer, the construction of the railway could begin. John Metcalfe of Bradford was appointed contractor and the first sod was eventually cut on Shrove Tuesday, 1864.

There were various difficulties with terrain and weather, chapels being undermined and collapsing and even, legend has it, a cow eating the plans of the railway! Eventually the line was completed and opened in 1867.

Mytholmes tunnel (left) and the old Mytholmes Lane Bridge over the beck (centre). The old line of the railway can be seen to the right of the tunnel with the old railway bridge under Mytholmes Lane just visible in the middle distance, *c.* 1910 [KLS]

As the line is now a preserved steam railway, its story is well documented and needs no further telling here. Some details of the effects that the railway's construction had on the Haworth landscape are less well known. As has already been mentioned Station Road, Oxenhope was made by the railway company. This can clearly be seen in the construction of the bridge which carries the road over Leeming Water which is typical railway work. Oxenhope station and goods yard are built where a couple of fields stood in the confluence of the Moorhouse Beck and Leeming Water. Close by was the old Oxenhope corn mill, now demolished. The site of the mill pond is now the station's overflow car park. There is a pleasant footpath down the valley from this car park to Haworth which follows the Bridgehouse Beck and the railway quite closely. Nearly half-way to Haworth the path crosses the Donkey Bridge and passes through North Ives plantation. Here one can see the old river course on the west side of the railway embankment, the stream now running in a straightened channel on the other side of the line. Nearer to Haworth, below Woodlands, the stream has again been straightened. It is now confined to the east side of the railway where it used to meander across the valley floor.

The carriage drive from Woodlands has a branch which crosses the railway line by a private bridge leading into the Bridgehouse Mill yard. This was one of the concessions which the railway had to make to R.S. Butterfield who lived at Woodlands and owned the mill. Just upstream from this bridge the line passes through the site of the Bridgehouse Mill pond mentioned in Chapter 2. At Bridgehouse Lane a complex series of changes took place. The turnpike road, which used to pass directly in front of the mill, was diverted a little to the north onto its present line and the new bridge was built over the stream and the railway line. The Woodlands carriage drive and Ivy Bank Lane were also diverted, bringing them above the Belle Isle cottages – they used to pass between the cottages and the stream. From Bridgehouse to the station there has been much change – the stream straightened, the valley bottom filled with rubble and the goods yard and Station Road constructed on the newly raised ground surface.

Perhaps the greatest change wrought by the coming of the railway has been the development of Haworth Brow. Where in the 1850s there were a few cottages and farms, there is now a thriving settlement which is practically a separate village from the old Haworth. The plots of land on which the new streets were built were sold at auction in 1877 – ten years after the railway opened. It seems probable that it was the new trade opportunities which the railway brought which necessitated all this new housing.

One loss occasioned by the railway's revival was the old Haworth corn mill. This used to stand in the corner of the goods yard but was demolished about thirty years ago.

Passing downstream, the next change to be noted is a reduction in size of the Ebor Mill pond. A little way downstream from Ebor Mill the railway enters Mytholmes Tunnel. This was not built until 1892 when the railway was re-routed to do away with the 1867 trestle bridge which crossed the Vale Mill pond and the river. A complex series of changes was occasioned by the making of the tunnel. Lower Mytholme farm was lost and Mytholmes Lane was re-routed. Traces of these changes can be found in an old bridge across Bridgehouse Beck leading nowhere and the nearly buried railway bridge by which Mytholmes Lane crossed the old line.

five

Water and Gas

Mention has already been made of two major civil engineering works – the Hebden Bridge Road and the Worth Valley Railway. However the most ambitious construction programme in the township was the creation of two great systems of reservoirs to supply Keighley and Bradford with water.

The newly formed Haworth Local Board of Health made a small reservoir in the fields above the parsonage in the 1850s. This was an attempt to deal with an intolerable situation. People either had to drink from wells which were contaminated with raw sewage and seepage from the burial ground or they had to fetch river water from a distance of half a mile or so. Not all residents were in favour of the board's attempts to rectify the situation. Some of the better-off already had piped water from a private scheme and did not see why they should pay rates to provide their poorer neighbours with the same benefit. Despite the opposition, the Church Hills reservoir was built by 1858 and can still be seen below Dimples Lane. It was not long before this proved inadequate for the village's needs but it took until 1881 before a second reservoir was completed. This is the Hough reservoir which, with its buttressed wall, is seen prominently from the Bankfield car park. Both of these small reservoirs were fed by springs. Both also had recurrent problems with leaks and each had to be substantially repaired or rebuilt. The Hough dam saw first its east wall and then its south wall collapse shortly after completion. The buttresses seen today were added to hold up the east wall. The south wall finally collapsed again in 1966, sending over half a million gallons of water flooding through the Sun Street area. Since then it has stood empty and derelict. Even after the construction of the second small reservoir water supplies were inadequate and intermittent. In 1891 Haworth made an arrangement to buy such water as it may require from Keighley's reservoirs at a favourable rate.

Whilst Haworth was struggling with its own small schemes, the neighbouring towns of Keighley and Bradford were both looking to the upper Worth Valley to supply their much greater needs for water. There was a conflict of interests here and competing schemes were submitted to Parliament. By the end of the 1860s a sensible agreement was reached by which Bradford took water from the Oxenhope Valley and Keighley took its share from the Worth Valley proper.

Under the provisions of the Bradford and Keighley Water Works Acts of 1869, a number of large supply and compensation reservoirs and several miles of conduits were built. Keighley's scheme in the Worth Valley called for a high-level supply reservoir at Water Sheddles and a compensation reservoir at Ponden. There was also provision for a further pair of reservoirs at Bully Trees and Lower Laithe for the low-level supply. The high-level scheme was completed by 1878 but construction of the low-level scheme was postponed for many years.

Water Sheddles reservoir supplies Keighley with water and holds some 191 million gallons. The reservoir lies wholly in Lancashire although it is on the Yorkshire side of the watershed. This is the result of an alteration to the county boundary which was made in 1618 at the instigation of the Duchy of Lancaster. The change was opposed by the commoners of Oakworth who, unsurprisingly as their opponent was King James I, lost their case. One result of this case was that Keighley had to pay rates to Lancashire for its reservoir.

As Water Sheddles sits almost at the highest point of the Worth Valley, it has very little direct catchment area and most of its water reaches it by an ingenious system of catchwater drains. The southern drain takes water from the head of Ponden Clough by a handsome pair of castle-like intakes. The water is then carried in a covered channel eastwards to Upper Ponden and then westwards to the reservoir. The route of this conduit lies along the waterworks road in Ponden Clough as far as Upper Ponden and thence across rough moorland to Water Sheddles. This part of its route can be followed as a faint footpath across the moor. A number of minor intakes and drains can be seen on the surface and there is a substantial stone aqueduct at Whitestone Clough. On Oakworth Moor to the north there is a vigorous spring which is captured by a second conduit and conveyed westwards to the reservoir. This channel is also covered and is difficult to follow as it soon leaves the open moor and traverses cultivated fields. A third source of water is Water Sheddles Clough which drains the Great Moss. This flows into a deep pool on the north side of the road and passes through a tunnel under the road to discharge into the reservoir well below the normal water level. There are open channels on both the north and south sides of the reservoir to carry floodwater past the reservoir. The northern channel crosses under the road twice in the length of the reservoir. The purpose of the floodwater channels is to prevent heavy loads of sediment being carried into the reservoir which might cause it to silt up. The water in the floodwater channels is carried round either end of the dam by the two bye-wash channels into the river. At the south end of the dam is an overflow sill which prevents the water rising above a safe level. Any excess water runs over this sill and into the southern bye-wash channel.

The connections between the various conduits feeding water into the reservoir and the floodwater channels are of great complexity. It is only by visiting Water Sheddles in time of drought that the details can be observed. The point at which the northern catchwater drain feeds into the reservoir eluded me for years until I realised that it runs directly beneath the northern floodwater channel as it passes under the road near the dam. An attempt is made to display these complicated arrangements in the accompanying diagram.

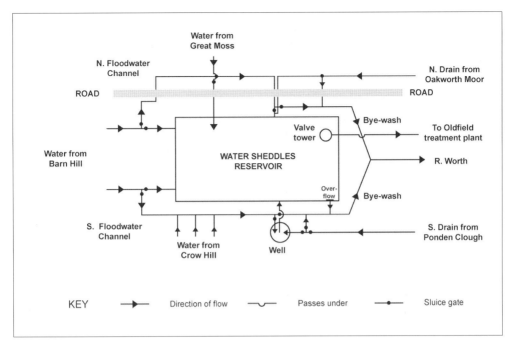

Diagrammatic plan of Water Sheddles reservoir.

A valve tower near the dam allows water to be drawn from the reservoir and piped to the water treatment plant at Oldfield near Oakworth and thence to a service reservoir at Black Hill above Keighley.

The mill owners of the Worth Valley had to be compensated for the water which was being diverted from the river for the reservoir. This was done by making a second reservoir at Ponden. This is filled by water running down Ponden Clough and the Worth – arrangements being made for at least one third of the water to enter the compensation reservoir. Ponden is a much simpler reservoir than Water Sheddles. Water enters directly from the streams at the head of the reservoir and there is no floodwater channel. A bye-wash takes surplus water round the dam and a valve tower permits water to be released into the river as required. The mill owners had complete control of the release of water from the reservoir to drive their water-wheels.

Both of these reservoirs are made with earthen embankment dams, as are all the reservoirs in the area. These are constructed with a watertight wall of clay in the middle and massive banks of stone and earth at either side. It can be seen that the outer slope is around 1 in 3, the inner slope is usually less steep and the toe of the embankment lies far out into the reservoir.

Before agreement had been reached with Bradford about the division of the waters of the Worth Valley, Keighley had proposed to build a further pair of reservoirs on Leeshaw water. Amongst the objectors to this proposal were the proprietors of the Worth Valley Railway. They pointed out that the stream below these two reservoirs flowed under both the Oxenhope and Haworth stations by archways. They were clearly nervous at the thought of millions of gallons of

Lower Laithe reservoir under construction. The timbered puddle trench at the centre of the embankment forms the main feature of this view, *c.* 1920.

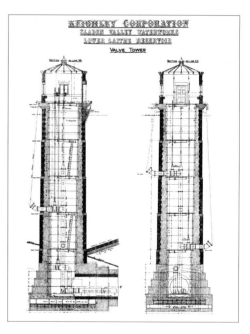

Above left: Lower Laithe reservoir's valve tower. [SCW]

Above right: Sectional drawings of the Lower Laithe valve tower, 1912.

water being impounded by earthen dams upstream of these stations. They expressed the fear that if there were any failure of the dams, 'water would rush down upon the railway … and seriously damage, if not destroy, the stations …'. It may be thought that they were exaggerating their fears to extract some kind of compensation from Keighley Corporation – until it is remembered that it was only five years previously that the Dale Dyke dam near Sheffield had failed causing the loss of 270 lives and some £300,000 worth of damage to property. Fortunately no such dam collapse has ever occurred in the Worth Valley but two of the local reservoirs (Leeming and Leeshaw) did give cause for concern in the 1870s and required remedial work.

Keighley never gave up its scheme for a low-level water supply in the Worth Valley. This was originally intended to comprise two reservoirs on the Sladen Beck – a supply reservoir at Bully Trees and a compensation reservoir at Lower Laithe. The geology of the valley proved unsatisfactory for this plan and a single reservoir fulfilling both functions was created instead. This is the Lower Laithe or Sladen reservoir below Stanbury village. Work did not start until 1912 and was much disrupted by the First World War. Work was finally finished in 1925 and the new reservoir was opened by the Marquis of Hartington in that year. Lower Laithe is a simple reservoir fed directly by the stream and having a single floodwater channel and bye-wash. At the head of the reservoir the stream enters a small settling pool, or residuum lodge, and from this the water passes into the head of the floodwater channel. Here there is a clever contrivance known as a leaping weir. In essence this consists of a metal plate spanning the width of the floodwater channel. Across the full width of this plate is a slot a few inches wide. When flow rates are normal the water drops through the slot into a short tunnel which leads into the head of the reservoir. If the stream is in spate the velocity of the water carries it straight over the slot and it passes down the floodwater channel thus preventing excessive amounts of silt from entering the reservoir. As at Water Sheddles, the dam is protected by an overflow sill which allows excess water to escape from the reservoir into the head of the bye-wash. From here all floodwater and overflow is conducted round the end of the dam in the bye-wash channel and returned to the stream below the dam. The diagram of this reservoir, which is fairly typical, may be compared with that for Water Sheddles above.

Bradford's water works in the Oxenhope Valley were built around the same time as Water Sheddles and Ponden. The foregoing description of the Keighley reservoirs covers many of the features to be seen in Victorian water storage systems. There is, however, one feature which is far more prominent in Bradford's scheme. This is the catchwater drain. Whilst those associated with Water Sheddles are mainly covered and inconspicuous, those which feed Bradford's reservoirs make striking features in the landscape. Two four-mile-long catchwater drains carry water from the upper reaches of the Oxenhope Valley into the Thornton Moor and Stubden reservoirs. The upper conduit which runs into Thornton Moor reservoir is now open as a footpath and can be readily inspected. It is well worth looking at the places where streams cross the conduit to see the various ingenious ways in which these junctions are contrived. Surplus water from the Thornton Moor conduit is passed down the hill to the Stubden conduit and from there down to Leeming reservoir. Leeming and Leeshaw are the two compensation reservoirs which provided water to power the mills of Oxenhope whose water supply was being diverted to Bradford. Each

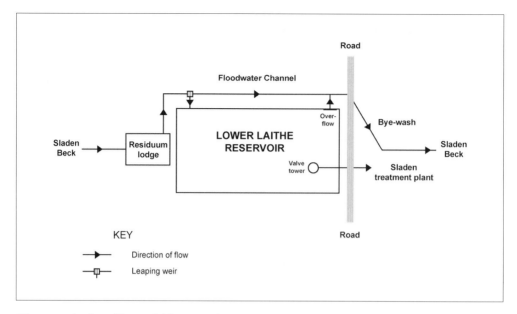

Diagrammatic plan of Lower Laithe reservoir.

of these reservoirs has its own catchwater drain of around a mile in length. Leeshaw's water is drawn from Rag Clough Beck whilst Leeming's catchwater starts at a spring just off the Hebden Bridge road above St Mary's church. It is not unknown for the wall surrounding this spring to be mistaken for a pinfold. Looking to the east from this point the course of the conduit is marked across the fields by a double row of stone markers. The purpose of these stones must often cause puzzlement to those travelling out of Oxenhope on the Cock Hill road. The Stubden, Leeming and Leeshaw catchwater drains pass through cultivated land and are not readily accessible. They are, however, broadly similar to the Thornton Moor conduit.

Thornton Moor reservoir itself is rather different from the other reservoirs in Haworth Township. Whereas most of these reservoirs are made by building a dam across the valley of a stream, that at Thornton Moor is not in a valley. It is perched on a hill side and the water is impounded by earth banks on three sides. One result of this design is that the reservoir has virtually no natural catchment area and nearly all its water is brought by the catchwater drain from the adjoining Oxenhope Valley.

The reservoirs and associated works in the upper Worth Valley are a remarkable, though little remarked, testament to the talents of the Victorian civil engineer.

Water is impounded in reservoirs on high ground and flows under gravity to the point of use. Gas, on the other hand, is lighter than air and flows upwards – hence the gas works are to be sought in the lowest part of the area supplied.

The earliest gas works in Haworth were those at a number of mills which made their own gas for lighting. Griffe, Ebor, Bridgehouse and Hollings Mills are all thought to have had small gas works. In 1845 gas street lighting was introduced to Haworth when the vestry agreed to purchase surplus gas from William Thomas at Hollings Mill and later from Butterfield of Bridgehouse Mill. These arrangements proved inadequate and the Haworth Gas Company was formed in 1857 to provide gas for domestic use as well as street lighting. After sites at Ivy Bank Lane and Belle Isle Lane were considered and rejected, the works were built at Mill Hey on land bought from William Thomas. The old gas pipes in the village were bought from the Thomases for £240 and extra pipes were laid.

Gas was first made in October 1857 but there were problems in getting the gas holder to rise. Extra weights were put on the chains to pull the holder up, thus creating a partial vacuum in the gas holder. Knowing that gas had been made, but unaware of the problems, one of the directors – James Lambert of Hall Green – decided to give his neighbours a demonstration of the new gas. He removed the cover from a valve at Hall Green and put a light to it. When asked what he was doing, he replied: 'Ah'm bahn to cap t'natives.' It is probable that Lambert himself was every bit as 'capped' as the natives when, owing to the reduced pressure in the system, the flame burnt back along the pipes and the gas holder exploded. One man was struck by a falling piece of metal and severely injured; the newspaper report of the incident concluded: 'We are glad to hear however that some hopes are held out of his recovery.' The gas holder was repaired at a cost of about £40 but of the fate of the injured man we hear nothing more.

Haworth Gas Works, *c.* 1960. From left: Retort house with chimney, small gas holder, purifier sheds, large gas holder – 'Ackroyd's Monument'. [KLS]

After this early setback the affairs of the company appear to have run more smoothly. In 1871 the gas works were purchased by the Haworth Local Board for £6,500. At some time in this period a second small gas holder was added but was only used until 1886 when a larger holder was built. This 1886 extension of the gas works was overseen by James Ackroyd as chairman of Haworth UDC. The new gas holder was jocularly referred to as Ackroyd's Monument. For half a century the Local Authority ran a cheap gas policy and the prices charged were little above the cost of production – Haworth had the cheapest gas in Yorkshire.

Gas was last made in Haworth in 1954. The accompanying photograph of the works at about that time shows the retort house, purifying sheds and gas holders. In the first of these was a series of horizontal retorts in which coal was heated to produce gas. In the open-sided purifier sheds tar, ammonia and hydrogen sulphide were removed. Finally the gas was stored in the two surviving gas holders.

After 1954 gas was piped up from the Keighley gas works at Thwaites. There was, at first, widespread prejudice against Keighley gas, which was held to be delivered at too low a pressure. The story is told of an old farmer at the Marsh in Oxenhope who went to milk his cow whilst he left a pan of sausages frying for his supper. When he returned the cat had eaten the sausages and was curled up asleep in the frying pan! In 1972 natural gas was introduced and the Haworth gas works finally closed. The site is now a car park.

six

Houses

Haworth today is principally a product of the nineteenth century, although there are some examples of earlier buildings. The pre-historic and medieval periods have left but slight and equivocal traces in the area. The earliest surviving building in the township is almost certainly the base of the church tower, which may well date to a rebuilding of 1488. Apart from this there are no buildings earlier than the seventeenth century. Although it cannot compare with Calderdale's rich heritage of old houses, Haworth does have a number of good houses from the 1600s.

In the village of Haworth there is Townend Farm on North Street, a cottage on Changegate dated 1671, the Old Hall at the bottom of Main Street and Old Fold Hall tucked away down Fern Street. There are others scattered about the township – Oxenhope's Mouldgreave and Stanbury's Ponden Hall being particularly fine examples.

Many of these older buildings have been restored in recent decades after having declined in fortunes earlier in the twentieth century. Townend Farm is an example of a sensitively restored early seventeenth-century farmhouse. It is of T-shaped plan and is most unusual in having an end cross-passage. This type of plan is rare and nearly all known examples are in the Burnley area across the border in Lancashire. The front elevation of this house has mullioned windows with arched tops and a four-centred arch door-head. Next door to the farmhouse is its barn; this was incorporated into a small textile mill and the whole is now a mill shop. Townend Farm formed a part of the Emmott estate and was for many years tenanted by the Binns family. The Binnses were farmers and carriers, they also provided horses to pull the Haworth fire engine which was kept in the old village lock-up across the road.

Around the corner from Townend is the Manor House more properly known as Cook Gate, one of Haworth's better eighteenth-century houses. Cook Gate itself is a good double-fronted house with ball finials, simple sash windows and a Georgian-style doorway with pilasters and pediment. Attached to this house is a cottage which must have formed part of an earlier

Town End Farm, *c.* 1900. [TJL]

seventeenth-century manor house. This has, unfortunately, been spoiled by heavy-handed alterations. Cook Gate came into the possession of the Midgley family by marriage in the mid-sixteenth century. A century or so later the Midgleys bought the Manor of Haworth. It was from this purchase in 1672 that Cook Gate became the Haworth Manor House. The Midgleys seem to have lived at Cook Gate on and off into the late eighteenth century and probably built the present house. When the manor was sold to Edward Ferrand of Bingley in 1811, Cook Gate was described as 'a good modern-built well-finished Stone House, with a Wool Warehouse, Barn, Stable and other Out-Buildings' and had thirty-nine acres of land. The most famous eighteenth-century house in Haworth is, of course, the Parsonage which was built by the Revd John Richardson around 1780. It is very similar in style to Cook Gate.

Old Fold Hall, which is mentioned above as an early seventeenth-century building, was re-fronted in 1724. This front, on Clarendon Street, is a good example of early eighteenth-century building materials and styles. The stone of the walls is a thin flag stone and the mullions and door lintels are also of flags 4 or 5 inches thick. A later change to thicker mullions (of around 6 inches) seems to reflect a major shift in quarrying techniques which took place around the early nineteenth century. Buildings later than about 1800 are readily recognisable by the thicker stone used in their construction – most obviously in the mullions.

Eighteenth-century workers' cottages are rather uncommon in the Haworth area and those that survive are often much altered. One of the better examples is to be found at the bottom

Eighteenth-century weavers' cottages, Butt Lane. [SCW]

of Butt Lane, just across the footbridge from the railway station. Here is a short row of weavers' cottages which were built around 1750 and raised to three storeys at the end of the century. They display the characteristic thin flag stone walling and 4-inch wide mullions of the eighteenth-century vernacular. The windows at the left-hand end of the row are of the multi-light variety commonly associated with handloom weavers' cottages. The windows in the rest of the row are of the squarer form typical of the first half of the nineteenth century – they were probably changed when the third storey was added. There are some traces of eighteenth-century construction in Haworth Main Street (e.g. No. 35) but most of the houses are nineteenth century.

Nos 25-27 Main Street represent a fine example of early nineteenth-century weaver's cottages. The stone used is thicker than the old flagstone style and the mullions are almost 6 inches wide. The multi-light weaver's window is still evident but the individual lights are now larger and squarer than those of the previous century.

At the left-hand end of the second floor windows is a taking–in door. These doors allowed heavy bales of yarn and bolts of cloth to be moved in and out of the workshop.

The typical worker's cottage of the first half of the nineteenth century is similar in style but smaller. Usually the buildings have two storeys and the windows only two or three lights. Many examples may be seen in various parts of Haworth and in other villages in the Worth Valley. Very good examples can be seen at 26-30 Sun Street, this is a row of three cottages dating from about 1830. Sometimes there is a cellar dwelling under the cottage, usually entered from an area

Nineteenth-century cottages in Changegate, 1967. [HH/KLS]

below street level. Good examples are to be found on West Lane. The finest cellar dwelling in the village was until recently preserved unaltered in Fern Street. The small-paned windows and other details have now been lost to modernisation.

After about 1850 housing in Haworth, as elsewhere, is post-vernacular – that is it follows standard designs and is less characteristic of the locality. There are significant areas of mill workers' cottages from this period in Coldshaw and the Brow.

Two important areas of nineteenth-century workers' housing were lost to ill-advised town clearance in about 1970. These were in the Changegate-North Street area and to the east of Main Street in an area variously known as Gauger's Croft, Brandy Row and Old Piccadilly. These were substantial groups of houses of the first half of the nineteenth century.

All the surviving early nineteenth-century houses in Haworth have, of course, been modernised but it is possible to build up a reasonable picture of the interior of such a house. Most would have had either one or two ground-floor rooms and two (or maybe three – there being no bathroom) first-floor chambers.

The main room on the ground floor was known as the 'house' and was used for cooking and eating as well as being the principal living room. In the early part of the nineteenth century an

Cellar dwelling, Fern Street. [SCW]

Left: Later nineteenth-century housing, Cold Street, *c.* 1930. [KLS]

Below: Demolition of nineteenth-century houses at Brandy Row, *c.* 1970. [TJL]

Kitchen range and set pot in wash kitchen, Bridgehouse Lane. [SCW]

open fireplace would have been used for heating and for cooking. A hinged arm known as a crane was attached above the fire and from this pans were suspended over the fire by 'reckons'. The occasional joint of meat could be cooked using a jack – a clockwork spit which hung from the reckon and turned the meat before the fire. The diet consisted very largely of oatmeal prepared either as porridge or as havercake. The latter is a type of bread made by pouring a thin oatmeal batter onto a heated stone slab. These 'bakestones' were generally made of a particular type of shale quarried near Delph in Saddleworth. The Delph bakestones were peddled over a wide area by men travelling with packhorses. There is field name evidence for bakestones having been quarried in Stanbury at one time but the Saddleworth trade wiped out all such local efforts at an early period. The monotony of this diet was remembered into the twentieth century. Timothy Feather, the Stanbury handloom weaver, is quoted as saying, 'Aw eyt porridge mornin, noon an neet.' One visitor to Timmy Feather did find him cooking potatoes for his supper though. More recently there is the story of a family in Haworth who often used to offer meals to an elderly neighbour which were gratefully received. Once, however, the daughter of the house was sent to ask if the old neighbour would like some porridge – 'Nay Eunice, love, till ah were wed aw et nowt but porridge – I couldn't look a plate o'porridge in t' face to this day.' In addition to the havercake or porridge there would be bacon (many cottagers kept pigs), milk, eggs and a few vegetables. By about 1850 cast-iron ranges were supplanting the open fire for heating and cooking. The cottage range provided hot plates, an oven and a supply of hot water.

Beside the hearth or range, furniture would be minimal – a table and chairs, a chest of drawers, a meal ark in which the oatmeal was stored, maybe a clock and a 'breead-flaik'. This was a wooden rack suspended from the ceiling over which oatcakes were hung to dry like so many dishcloths. Similar racks are still sometimes used for drying clothes. Artificial lighting would be used as little as possible. Until about 1860 the only sources of light would be tallow candles or rushlights. Rushlights were the pithy insides of the common rush dipped in tallow. They gave an adequate light for a small cottage and were cheap. Wax candles did not become readily available until paraffin wax was introduced around 1860 and they were expensive. By this time gas lighting was a possibility, the Haworth Gas Company having started operations in 1857. Early gas lights were simple jets on wall brackets, the gas mantle came towards the end of the century. In these early years gas lighting would be the privilege of the better-off but all would benefit from gas street lighting which remained in use until around 1965. Cooking by gas would have been a much later introduction into working-class houses.

Left: Bill Parker, lamplighter, Mill Hey, *c.* 1960. [WEP]

Opposite: Rear of Robert Lambert's shop, Main Street. Babbage Report, 1850. [KLS]

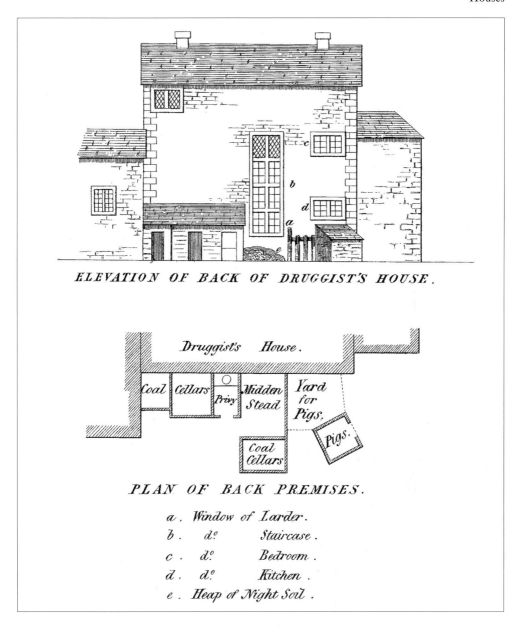

ELEVATION OF BACK OF DRUGGIST'S HOUSE.

PLAN OF BACK PREMISES.

a . Window of Larder.
b . d.º Staircase.
c . d.º Bedroom.
d . d.º Kitchen.
e . Heap of Night Soil.

If there was a second room on the ground floor it would have been a scullery or wash-kitchen. This would be equipped with a set pot and slop stone. The set pot was a large iron pot built into a stone or brick surround over a small hearth. It was used to heat large quantities of water for the weekly wash or for making sheep's head broth and the like. The slop stone was a large, shallow stone sink in which the washing up was done; they are still occasionally to be seen in some older houses. Washing was done in a dolly tub with a posser and much hard labour. Some houses had the wash kitchen located in a separate out-building.

Most nineteenth-century cottages had a small keeping cellar which had stone shelves ('cooil benks') round the walls and sometimes a stone-built table in the middle. They were used for food storage. The keeping cellar is sometimes external to the house in the more rural areas. A number of examples survive in the Haworth area; these are sometimes referred to as ice-houses but they are not – just simple food storage areas.

A good proportion of the cellars under eighteenth- and nineteenth-century cottages in Haworth have barrel-vaulted roofs. These have probably contributed to the persistent tales of secret tunnels running from the church to the Old Hall and thence to the Bridgehouse area. Such romantic stories are generally without foundation and there is no evidence to substantiate these claims.

The first-floor chambers would be used as bedrooms and also as workshops before weaving moved into the mills. Sometimes one can see slots cut into the beams of these rooms where the handloom was fixed. Wool combing was also carried out in the house, a very unhealthy proceeding. The sleeping arrangements would be crowded – the younger children sleeping with their parents, the older ones generally in a separate room. If it was possible there would probably be some attempt to segregate boys and girls in their teenage years. Quite small houses were built with three bedrooms in the second half of the nineteenth century. There was room to make three small bedrooms because there was no bathroom. Bathing was done rather infrequently by today's standards, in a tin bath in front of the fire with water heated in the set pot.

Sanitation generally was a problem in Haworth in the nineteenth century. Conditions were so bad in 1850 that an inspector was sent from London to make a report. Benjamin Herschel Babbage, the son of Charles Babbage who is remembered as the father of the computer, spent three days in Haworth and produced a damning account of the village's water supply and sewerage – or lack of it. The Babbage Report has often been quoted for its descriptions of filthy privies shared by two dozen families, water that even the cattle refused to drink and houses rendered almost uninhabitable by adjoining pigsties and stinking, overflowing middens. What is less often realised is that the Local Board of Health was unable to make much headway against such nuisances until much later in the century. John Milligan investigated the sanitary condition of the Worth Valley in 1873. His report on Haworth does not survive but his account of some privies in Oxenhope may be taken as representative of conditions in the area:

> The privy at the top of the row was of the kind usually seen in this district, built of rough unplastered and uncemented fence stones, without door, and with a large pit full of ashes, potato parings, and house rubbish, open to rain and moisture. The middle one is a similar primitive affair, the only seat being the branch of a tree laid crossways, on which the unfortunate tenants must perch.

In Leeming, Milligan described twenty houses occupied by reservoir navvies which were served by '*one* dirty, seatless, almost unapproachable little privy'. He recommended that all who have the leisure should visit this 'acme and summit of unsanitary bliss'.

seven

Shops and Inns

Haworth Main Street today has a great many shops but few which cater for those who live in the village. The vast majority are aimed squarely at the large numbers of visitors who are drawn by the Brontë connection, the preserved railway or who are just seeking an interesting day out. The grocers, butchers, chemists, newsagents and so on – the everyday shops which do cater for the residents – are mainly to be found away from the centre of the village. A number of these which serve the older part of the village are on Sun Street but the majority of them are on Mill Hey in the valley bottom.

It was not always so. Until quite recent times, certainly up to the 1950s, the Main Street was not swamped with 'Ye Olde' thises and 'Brontë' thats, but had the normal array of Co-ops, outfitters, shoe shops, grocers, butchers and post office that any large village needs.

Through the trade directories of the nineteenth century we can form some picture of how the number and range of retail businesses grew to cater for the expanding population of Haworth. Between 1821 and 1851 the population of the township grew by over 40% from 4,700 to 6,800. In 1822 there were eleven grocers, five butchers, three cabinet makers, two confectioners and one apiece of spirit merchants, plumbers, plasterers, braziers, ironmongers, watchmakers and whitesmiths. There are a few surprising omissions in this list, perhaps because trade directories were new and the early ones may have been less comprehensive than they were later to become. The first 'chymist' appears in 1828 in the person of Joseph Hardaker whom we shall meet later as one of Haworth's less well known literary figures. 1828 also saw the first mention of clog makers of whom there were three. The 1830s brought in boot makers, drapers, painters, tailors and various shopkeepers unspecified.

By the mid-century there were around ninety retailers and craftsmen listed in White's Directory of 1853. They were: blacksmiths (four), booksellers (two), boot makers (eleven), butchers (five), cabinet makers (seven), cloggers (six), cooper (one), drapers (two), dress maker (one), grocers (twenty-eight), hairdresser (one), ironmonger (one), painters (two), plasterers

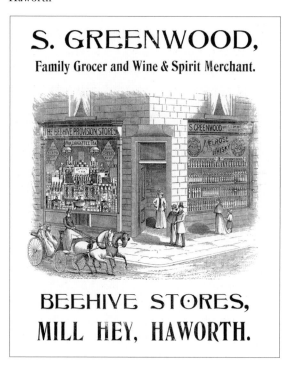

S. GREENWOOD,
Family Grocer and Wine & Spirit Merchant.

**BEEHIVE STORES,
MILL HEY, HAWORTH.**

Grocery shop on Mill Hey from an early advertisement, *c.* 1900.

(four), plumber (one), post office (one), surgeons (two), tailors (eight), tinner (one), wheelwrights (two), wine merchant (one). That this list is not complete is proved by the absence of the druggist whom we know to have been at the top of Main Street at this time. He is in fact in the directory but wrongly said to be in Oxenhope.

This druggist was called Robert Lambert and he is one of a family who were active in various trades in Haworth for most of the nineteenth century. The Lamberts provide an interesting example of a trade family and their activities will repay a closer look.

We first hear of Tobias (or Tobit) Lambert in 1800 when he and Frances Briggs were married at the parish church. He was born in Addingham about 1767; she was eight years younger and was born in Wilsden. Their first child, John, was born eight months later at Sowdens. The rest of their ten children were born in Haworth between 1802 and 1817. What brought the couple to Haworth and how they made their living up to 1814 we do not know. By 1814 Tobias had a house and shop next to the Fleece in Main Street and was described as a shop keeper. It was at Hall Green that Lambert was to establish the shop which remained in his family for most of the nineteenth century. Quite when this was we do not know but he certainly had considerable property there by 1819. He continued to acquire more land at Hall Green in the 1820s and '30s. By 1838 Lambert owned and occupied a house and shop, a glazier's shop and a comb shop at Hall Green. Lambert's grocer's shop at Hall Green is still in existence as a general store, and is now known as Sun Street Stores. The building appears to date from around 1820. It seems most likely that Tobias Lambert built himself a house and shop at Hall Green just before 1820 and moved his family and business there from Main Street.

The mention of a comb shop in 1838 alerts us to the fact that Lambert, along with his sons John and James, was involved in the textile industry. He was, in fact, one of the small clothiers who flourished in the days of handloom weaving. The trade directories from 1822 onwards describe him as a worsted manufacturer. He would have been buying wool from a stapler and putting it out to be combed by hand in cottages nearby. The tops were then taken to one of the local mills such as Bridgehouse or Ebor to be spun into yarn. Lambert delivered the yarn to weavers working in their own homes and finally collected the finished pieces from them. We know that he sold his cloth at the Bradford piece market, business continuing at the Bull's Head when the piece hall closed each day. When Lambert started in this business there was no competition from the mills, but the growing use of the power-loom in the 1840s and '50s must have made life increasingly difficult for the small clothiers. This is evidenced in the trade directory entries. Both Tobias and his eldest son John appear to have given up the textile business around 1848 each to concentrate on his grocery shop – Tobias at Hall Green and John in Main Street. John's younger brother James continued as a worsted manufacturer until 1856 after which he too became a grocer. No doubt this was partly because of the need for him to take on his father's shop after Tobias died in 1855. The end of the Lamberts' involvement in textile manufacture does, however, coincide with the triumph of the power-loom and the factory system. The story of the Lambert family is a very good example of the dual economy in action and clearly demonstrates the shift of textile manufacture from the cottage to the mill.

After they ceased to make cloth John and James Lambert continued to run their grocery shops until they retired. James gave up business in the mid-1870s and lived in retirement at the Old Hall opposite his shop until his death at the age of eighty-two. His elder brother John seems to have run his Main Street shop until his death at the age of eighty-five in 1886. The shop built by Tobias Lambert at Hall Green has now been a general grocery store for nearly 200 years – a remarkable example of continuity.

Two more of Tobias Lambert's sons established businesses in the village. It has already been mentioned that Robert had the druggist's shop at the top of Main Street (now 'The Apothecary'). He started in business around 1840 and there is a possibility that he took over the apothecary-poet Joseph Hardaker's shop when the latter became too ill to work. From what we know of Hardaker's business it is unlikely that he was in the rather handsome Main Street premises which Lambert occupied by 1850. Lambert dealt in groceries as well as medicines and perhaps built himself a new and larger shop in the 1840s. Robert continued to run his businesses until his death in 1882. His widow Betty ran the shop for a while after his death but she died herself in 1888. It is just possible that Betty is a link between Robert Lambert and Joseph Hardaker. In 1838 the druggist's shop was in the name of an Elizabeth Hardaker but unfortunately Robert did not marry in Haworth and we do not know his wife's maiden name.

Finally there was Thomas, the youngest of the four Lambert sons, who was a plumber. It will be recalled that Tobias Lambert had a glazier's shop amongst his property in 1838. In 1841 Thomas is described as a glazier and, no doubt, was working at his father's Hall Green premises. By 1851 he had married and moved to Changegate; he and his wife made a further move to West Lane by 1861. Thomas died some time after 1867 and his widow continued to run the

Townend Co-op, Main Street, formerly Robert Lambert's shop, 1963.

business for about another ten years with the help of her son, Tobias. The business was carried on at West Lane by younger members of the family until at least 1908.

Some mention should be made of the Haworth Co-operative Society which was a feature of village life for over a century. The society was formed in 1861 and rented a small shop in Main Street (now No. 11). The business grew rapidly with larger premises being acquired a little further up Main Street in 1866. A second (Townend) branch was opened at the end of that year. Further branches were opened in Stanbury and on the Brow in 1872 and 1881. A handsome new central store was opened in Main Street in 1898. By the time of the society's centenary in 1961 there were seven branches and a coal depot at the railway yard. The decline thereafter was rapid and within ten years Haworth Co-op was gone.

In one of the darker recesses of Keighley Reference Library there is a large old map. It consists of several sheets of the 1890s 6-inch OS map joined together and bears the title *Keighley and District Band of Hope Union Drink Map*. On it the pubs, beer houses, clubs, off-licences and confectioners are marked by various symbols in red and Sunday schools in blue.

Top: Haworth Co-operative Society, Main Street, *c.* 1910. [BS]

Above left: Haworth Co-operative Society, Main Street. From an early advertisement, *c.* 1900.

Above right: White Lion Inn, West Lane, *c.* 1893.

On the side of the angels, Haworth village had six Sunday schools of which three, all Methodist, were in the Band of Hope Union. These were outnumbered by a tide of licensed premises: seven public houses, three clubs that supplied drink, six off-licences and one confectioner. Leaving aside the rather odd inclusion of the confectioner (was it because they sold yeast?) this left sixteen premises selling alcoholic drink in the village.

It is odd that there are no beer houses shown on the map although they may all have either acquired full licenses or become off-licences by 1898 when the map was made. Beer houses, premises which did not sell spirits, were allowed to operate without the need for a full license and were introduced in 1830 to counter the menace of the gin palaces. They leave far less trace of their existence than inns but we do know that there were two in Haworth in 1834 and five by 1841. We know little about these beer shops but one was kept at the bottom of Changegate by William Parker from the 1830s to the 1850s. We know only two by name: the Belle Isle Inn which was at the corner of Bridgehouse Lane and Belle Isle Road and the Royal Oak on Mill Hey which started as a beer house but gained a full license around 1850.

Of the seven pubs two have long since gone – the New Inn on Sun Street, known apparently for its rat pie (a dish not often seen on today's bar menus), and the Cross at the top of Main Street. We know little of the early history of the inns but there were a dozen licensees in the township by 1723. It has been observed that any house in Haworth is about a hundred years younger than its owner believes it to be. This rule is doubly true of public houses which often claim to be seventeenth-century coaching inns – in a village which was not served by coaches! The first pub named in the records is the Black Bull in 1744, lending support to the suggestion that the oldest pub in any town is the one nearest the church. The Kings Arms is first named as the meeting place of the manorial court in 1763 but may have been used for that purpose from 1748. The coming of the turnpike road was probably critical to the growth of the more important inns in the village. The case of the White Lion may be taken as a typical example. It is first recorded in the property deeds in 1783 when it was called the Blue Bell. Clearly it was named after the Blue Bell Turnpike and was probably established soon after the road was opened in 1755. From 1796 to 1812 the Lion was a meeting place for Haworth's first Masonic lodge, the Prince George Lodge. In 1812 the lodge amalgamated with the Three Graces Lodge and meetings were continued at the Black Bull until the masons acquired their own premises on Newell Hill, now Lodge Street.

In 1850 the White Lion was bought by J. & R. R. Thomas who were wine and spirit merchants. They rebuilt the place around 1858, probably not before time – Babbage had described a scene of great squalor around the old building. In the late nineteenth century the Lion passed into the hands of Samuel Ogden who owned the Fallwood Brewery near the railway station. Haworth's other main brewery was Parker's Clarendon Brewery up Brow Road. Both date from the 1870s. Before this time the village's pubs would have brewed their own beer and brewhouses are mentioned in the early rating valuations.

eight

Church and Chapel

There is a story, much discussed by earlier antiquarians, that Haworth church goes back to the incredibly early date of AD 600. This is based on an inscription on the church tower, and another (now lost) within the church. Whittaker, in his *History of Craven*, dismissed the story as a misunderstanding as long ago as 1816, but it is often re-told. The Latin inscription – with English translation alongside – can be seen just above the sundial on the south wall of the tower. It looks to be of no great age and must be a copy of an earlier stone now lost.

More interesting is the possibility that there was a British church at Stanbury before the Augustinian conversion. At the western end of Stanbury village lying just north of the road to Colne are two fields with the name Eccles. This place name is held to be a good indicator of the presence of a pre-Saxon church. The nearby 'Hob' place names are also regarded as suggesting the presence of a British settlement in this area. In 1980 a number of Eccles sites in Yorkshire were investigated for abnormally high levels of phosphates in the soil. A positive result was obtained at Stanbury and this was thought to indicate the possible presence of a burial ground associated with the postulated British church. Unfortunately for this persuasive theory I have recently been able to show that the 'Eccles' field names at Stanbury are not recorded before 1850. In various documents from 1671 to 1838 the fields are called Aightalls or Aughtalls. It is easy to see how this could have been corrupted to 'Eccles'. The phosphate evidence remains to be explained as do certain crop marks in the lower 'Eccles' field which seem to show a rectangular enclosure of some kind. However the primary evidence has been shown to be spurious and there must now be serious doubt about any early church at Stanbury.

The first reliable mention of Haworth church is in 1317 when there is reference to its existence from 'ancient times'. Whenever the first church may have been built, there seems to have been a new church built in 1488. It is possible that the base of the church tower is a survival of this fifteenth-century church. We have little clue as to what the rest of this building was like but a simple, small, rectangular plan is likely. Around 1600 there was an enlargement of the church and this may well have been the addition of a half-width north aisle along the nave.

William Grimshaw, the great evangelical preacher, came to Haworth in 1742 and the resulting vast congregations made a further enlargement of the church necessary. It was not until 1755 that Grimshaw managed to collect sufficient money for the job – he had undertaken to raise the money without levying a church rate for the purpose. The enlargement of 1755 returned the church to a rectangular plan by lengthening and widening the north aisle and raised the height of both church and tower. The resulting building was about 63 feet by 44 feet with south and north aisles. Down the centre of the church was a row of octagonal columns which supported the roof. The disposition of the church furniture reflected the evangelical nature of Grimshaw's (and his successors') services. The three-decker pulpit and reading desk in the middle of the south wall was the main focal point, with relatively less prominence accorded to the communion table at the east end. The church was fitted with high-sided box pews entered by doors which bore the names of the sitting holders. Some of these pew doors can be seen in the school rooms on Church Street and in the Parsonage Museum. Grimshaw also raised the church tower at this time. After Grimshaw's death in 1763 there was still a shortage of space and galleries were added in 1779.

The addition of the galleries blocked much of the light from the windows and made the church rather dark. The communion table must have been in a very cramped situation between the pews and the east wall and under the organ loft. This proved so inconvenient to the Revd John Wade (who placed more emphasis on the sacrament than his predecessors) that he had the east gallery removed in 1870. Amongst other changes made at the time was the installation of a new clock. The church tower was once again raised to accommodate the dials. The successive raisings of the tower lead Keighley people to quip that Haworth folk 'mucked the church to make it grow'.

When one of the local mill owners, Michael Merrall, offered £5,000 towards the cost of a new church, Wade accepted gratefully. The old church was demolished in 1879 amidst much outcry from those who wished to see it preserved as a Brontë shrine. There was, at that time, a lot of talk as to the antiquity of the church which was being destroyed. An examination of the plans and photographs of the old church makes it seem likely that very little, apart from the tower, survived from before 1755. The new church was consecrated in 1881 and is that which exists today. It bears very little relation to the older churches on the site having only the base of the tower remaining from earlier times.

The furore over the demolition of the old church came largely from people outside Haworth who were motivated by a passionate regard for the Brontë sisters' writings. Whilst regretting the loss of the old church, one must have much sympathy with Mr Wade who saw the church as a place of worship – not of literary pilgrimage. Indeed the really important association that was lost received less attention at the time – that with William Grimshaw. Grimshaw had a profound effect upon the religious life not only of Haworth, but of the whole of northern England. Had he not died when he did he may very well have succeeded John Wesley as the leader of the Methodist church.

The parish church was not the only place of worship that Grimshaw built during his time in Haworth. It must be remembered that in Grimshaw's (and Wesley's) time the Methodist

The old church, Haworth, from a hymn sheet, early nineteenth century. [KLS]

Interior of the old church, c. 1870. The figures stand in the choir pews, the north gallery is on the left, the communion rails are visible below the organ.

connection was a movement within the Church of England. Both William Grimshaw and John Wesley died as Anglican ministers and the Methodists did not finally sever their connection with the established Church until 1795. Whilst a number of Anglican clergy were leading members of the Methodist movement and a good many were broadly sympathetic to the Methodists, there were many who were downright hostile. George White, vicar of the nearby Lancashire town of Colne, is a good example of the latter. He often incited drunken mobs to attack Methodist preachers in his parish and in 1748 John Wesley, William Grimshaw and a number of companions were seriously assaulted at Barrowford.

Grimshaw feared that such a man might eventually be appointed to the living at Haworth and wished to provide a haven for his Methodist followers to use should this happen. In 1757 he was left £140 towards the cost of building a Methodist chapel in Haworth. In the following two years he built a small chapel and preacher's house on West Lane. The Haworth Manor Court Rolls for 1758 show that Grimshaw paid a fine for building on 'lands encroached from the lord's waste'.

This first Methodist chapel in the township was a very modest building being only 36 feet by 27 feet. It was attached to the preacher's house and the whole cost was something over £200. This left a considerable sum of money to be found and one of Grimshaw's money-raising efforts was an investment in the State Lottery. This caused him much concern as to its propriety and was attended with scant success. Of the chapel only a fragment of wall remains which is attached to the surviving preacher's house – now a private dwelling locally known as the caretaker's cottage.

Grimshaw's fears as to his successor were unfounded, John Richardson proving an exemplary pastor who served the chapelry for twenty-seven years. A recollection of Richardson by one of his servants survives and makes clear that he was a conscientious clergyman who was well loved by his parishioners. It describes him thus:

a very handsome gentleman, and strong in appearance; generally dressed very neat, and wore a powdered wig, which was fashionable for clergymen at that time, similar to what is now worn by judges and barristers at this day, and he mostly wore a clerical three-cornered hat, and wore his bands regularly on week days, when visiting his parishioners. He was never married, except to his Church and his people. In his time there was a favourite spot, named Folly Spring, in the valley, adjoining Bridge house, which had one of the strongest springs in the locality, and where a convenient place once stood, as a place to undress in for bathing purposes. In summer time he often bathed in that crystal spring of water.

Folly Spring is now lost amongst the mill ponds of Ivy Bank Mill but the whole area is still locally known as Folly.

Perhaps because Richardson proved to be such a satisfactory successor to Grimshaw the need for a separate Methodist chapel does not seem to have been felt and the 1758 building does not appear to have been much used. By the 1770s the chapel was more or less derelict and was rebuilt around 1790. The ground floor was converted into cottages and the Methodists met in the upper room. Their fortunes in Haworth then started to grow and enlargements of the chapel were undertaken in 1805 and again in 1822.

West Lane Methodist chapel and Sunday School, *c.* 1910. [KLS]

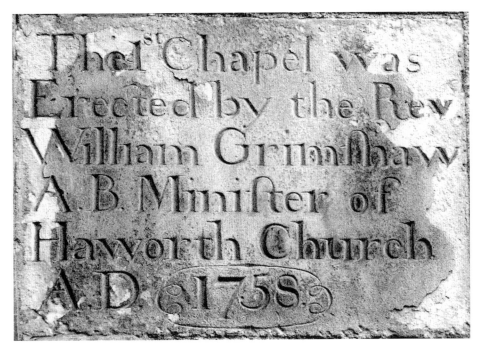

West Lane Methodist chapel date stone. Note how the wording has been changed from 'This Chapel' to 'The 1st Chapel'. [SCW]

West Lane Baptist chapel and manse. [SCW]

The development of the West Lane Methodist Chapel buildings in the mid-1800s becomes rather complex and has been the subject of misunderstandings. A Sunday school building was added in 1830. The substantially remodelled old chapel building was replaced in 1845 by a new chapel in the style of James Simpson of Leeds. This new building held a congregation of 650 and had an organ installed in 1847.

It is often said that the chapel was enlarged in 1853 but what almost certainly happened in that year is that the original Sunday school building was demolished and replaced by a larger new building. Apart from occasional renovations, this remained the situation for the next century. Declining congregations and increased costs led to the demolition of the chapel building in 1951, the Sunday school being redesigned to serve as both chapel and school. Thus the building which is used today is the second Sunday school building, erected in 1853 and the most recent erection on the site. Just a few yards towards Main Street stands the old preacher's house with a small section of wall which reminds us of Grimshaw's original chapel of 1758.

A little further on is the West Lane Baptist Chapel representing the other main non-conformist denomination active in the village. Its building history is not unlike that of the Methodist chapel along the street. In fact it is difficult to avoid the feeling that each group was peering over its walls at the activities of its neighbour: 'Ee! look what that lot's up to nah. We mun get agate o' buildin' ageean!' Of course such thoughts would be unworthy and no doubt the building programmes were driven by far more serious considerations!

Hall Green Baptist chapel, 1824, from an early engraving.

The first Baptist meetings in Haworth Township were held at North Ives, which was licensed as a preaching house in 1693. One of Grimshaw's converts, James Hartley, became a Baptist and gathered a group to worship in Haworth. The first chapel on West Lane was built in 1752. This became unsafe and was demolished in 1775, a larger and higher-walled chapel being built in its place. This in its turn outlived its usefulness and was replaced by the present chapel building in 1845. The 1775 building was not demolished until around 1860, being used as a Sunday school until then. A new Sunday school was added on to the back of the chapel building in 1859 and a primary school was added on to the back of that in 1909. Like many chapel congregations, the West Lane Baptists were faced with increasing problems in maintaining their buildings with declining numbers and in 1997 parts of the building were converted for housing and more houses were built in its grounds. This secured the future of the chapel, which continues to be used both for worship and for a number of community groups.

These West Lane chapels were by no means the only non-conformist chapels in Haworth. The Baptists suffered a schism over music in the early nineteenth century with the secessionists building a new chapel at the top of Bridgehouse Lane. The Hall Green chapel, as it is called, was built in 1824 and is the oldest surviving place of worship in Haworth. It too maintains an active life today. There were also Primitive and Wesleyan Methodist chapels at the bottom of the Brow. The Salvationists too had a citadel in Haworth for a good number of years. Finally a Roman Catholic church opened at Ebor Lane in the twentieth century.

nine

The Wise Man and the Horse Doctor

Somewhere in Haworth churchyard lies the body of John Kay, who was buried there in January 1847. There is no memorial inscription and it is impossible to know just where he lies – probably in that section of the graveyard which clusters densely round the parsonage garden. The funeral service was conducted by Patrick Brontë and one would give much to know what was going through Patrick's mind as he laid to rest Haworth's famous wise man. Kay's obituary states that he had been in the habit of attending morning services but had long ago given up, as 'the singularity of his avocation caused him to seek the utmost privacy'. Some light is, perhaps, cast on Kay's relations with Brontë by a story told in James Whalley's peculiar little book *The Wild Moor*. Two young ladies had come to Haworth to consult the famous wise man as to their future prospects and enquired the way to his house. They were taken to the parsonage by a servant girl who thought that 'the wisest man' must mean the parson. Here the two were treated by Patrick Brontë to a lecture on their foolishness and wickedness. Whalley has him cite Leviticus on the satanic inspiration of all such 'prognosticators'. Whalley is probably not to be taken too literally in this, or in his other accounts of Kay, but as an Anglican clergyman himself he is a good guide to the view which Patrick might have taken on the subject.

There are a number of references to Old Jack Kay and his magical practices in various books about the Haworth area written from the 1860s to the 1890s. These give us enough information about Kay's reputed powers to enable us to place him firmly in the wise man tradition of the eighteenth and nineteenth centuries. Drawing on accounts of other northern cunning folk of the period and on relics preserved in the local museum helps to fill out our picture of Kay and his activities.

It is clear from the written accounts of Jack Kay that he was held in high regard over a wide area in western Yorkshire and eastern Lancashire. He is said to have been consulted by both the

Portrait of Old Jack Kay the Haworth wise man,
c. 1840. [CR]

common folk and carriage folk of the district. The picture presented is of a serious-minded man who has learnt his herb and star lore by close study of the natural world and who considers his abilities to entail responsibilities.

From the scraps of information in the nineteenth-century sources it is clear that Kay had a reputation in most of the fields that one would expect of a village wise man. First came fortune-telling, particularly the ability to indicate the name, or appearance, of a future wife or husband. Astrology, scrying and reading from 'black art books' are mentioned as Kay's methods for this kind of divination. In a surviving portrait of Jack Kay he holds some kind of planetary chart and two occult books are on a shelf behind him. There is a fair amount of evidence for astrological belief and practice in the Haworth area. In the parish registers a 'storm of wind and hail' in 1652 was attributed to 'the Effects of the Conjunction of Saturn and Mars; those Planets being then supposed to be conjoined in the Sign of Leo'. At the end of August 1658 much damage was done by 'prodigious storms and tempests' and 'a great flood'. These were held to have been caused by Jupiter and Mercury and a conjunction of Saturn and, probably, Mars. In the Rush Isles commonplace-book (to which we shall come shortly) there is a natal chart dated 1798. A crystal ball, mirror or dish of water was commonly used by wise men to show the future – particularly a future lover or spouse. Kay's use of a crystal ball is mentioned more than once and may reasonably be assumed although it is not depicted in the portrait.

Secondly, we are told that Kay provided his clients with charms to avert ill fortune. Making these charms was a staple of the wise man's trade and scraps of paper or vellum bearing odd symbols and a few lines of debased Latin were commonly carried about the person or concealed within the house for protection. The Cliffe Castle collection contained a number of these charms and one of them (which now appears to be lost) was found under a floor at Westfield Farm in Oxenhope. This house was built around 1780 and so the charm may date from a generation or two before Jack Kay. It consisted of a small piece of paper, folded and sealed, bearing three symbols – very loosely like an X, W and reversed S. There were also five lines of pseudo-Latin doggerel of uncertain meaning. Other charms to protect against witchcraft were common and a few examples may still be seen on older houses. Witch stones (stones with a naturally occurring hole, suspended by a loop of thread), horseshoes and crosses of rowan twigs were commonly used. Close examination of older houses in the area will sometimes reveal a letter W carved on a door jamb – these too were for protection against witches. Presumably such charms could be contrived by the householder himself without recourse to the wise man.

There is an 1867 pamphlet by Keighley dialect poet Bill o'th' Hoylus End which contains the following verse about Jack Kay:

Here mony a silly lad hez been,
To knaw his futur life,
An thro' the magic glass hez seen
An knawn his future wife;
An so wi mony a timid lass,
Whose heead was rather shallow,
Hez paid ould Jack her bit o' brass
To see her futur fellor.

An poverty herself hez been,
To seek her refuge here,
To knaw the cause of all her woes,
An asks it wi a tear,
Who was the witch t' withered witch
That kept them all so poor;
An mony a cat hez paid for that,
Aback ot milkhus door.
A mother too, her son to know

If he wor slain in battle,
T' farmer wild was here beguil'd
Abaat his dying cattle;
An mony a poor ould wife wor blam'd,
An threatened by t' switch
Because she had a wrinkled brow,
They took her for a witch.

An mony a fooil fra Keighlee come
To hear his fortune read,
An t'silly ape would stare an gape,
An swollow all wor sed,
An paid his brass to look at glass,
An see his future bride;
Imaginin he saw her chin
An went home satisfied

Here we have the fortune-telling and the use of the crystal ball and, most importantly, the wise man's reputation for detecting and defeating witches. We also see that by 1867 the beliefs on which Kay's career was founded were dying out – Bill o'th' Hoylus was not an educated man and his scepticism is robustly obvious. The belief in witchcraft was the very core of the wise man's business – his principal function was to find the witch responsible for cursing a person or a man's cattle and to deal with her either directly or otherwise. A pamphlet published as late as 1956 gives us a memory of Kay's reputation in this field. In his *Autobiography* Thomas Wood (1822-1880) recalls how, in his childhood, illness in man and beast was often attributed to the evil eye. He records the case of a hitherto healthy young woman 'wasting away like a sweating candle' after being 'wished' – i.e. cursed by a witch. The neighbours gather round in serious, whispered consultation, in the dimly lighted room, 'doctor's stuff' is of no use they aver whilst the curse has a hold: 'Better go to Jack Kaye's he'll make t'auld witch squeak at's done it'.

A common way to make the witch squeak was the witch bottle. Hairs and nail parings and urine from the victim would be put in a bottle with pins, nails, thorns or other sharp objects. The closely sealed bottle was then either buried or placed on the fire. In either case the witch would be seized with violent pains in the bladder, which the bottle symbolized. Only by confessing her guilt and lifting the curse could she save herself. That this procedure was used in this area is evidenced by a witch bottle in the Cliffe Castle collection. The bottle was found buried under a cottage floor in the Trawden area, just over the Lancashire boundary from Haworth. It is a 6-inch tall glazed stoneware bottle and contained four nails, three pieces of a broken file, a ball of hair and some liquid – presumably urine.

If cattle were afflicted by a witch's curse the remedy was to take the heart of one of the victims and pierce it all over with nails or pins. The heart was then either burnt or hung in the chimney. Again the result was to inflict agony on the guilty witch until she was obliged to relent. Atkinson (*Forty Years in a Moorland Parish*, 1891) gives a detailed account of the procedure adopted on the North York Moors. A good, hot fire was built of elder wood and the doors and windows of the house were tightly sealed and covered. The heart of the deceased animal was stuck with nine new pins, nine new needles and nine new nails. Exactly at midnight the prepared heart was burnt to ashes in the fire accompanied by a specified reading from Psalms. Again the Cliffe Castle collection confirms the prevalence of this sort of practice in the area. The dried heart of a bullock stuck with dozens of pins was found under the floorboards of a house in Keighley.

There was one other main activity of wise men which is not mentioned in the accounts of Jack Kay and that was the discovery of thieves and the recovery of stolen or lost goods. He did, however, have a considerable reputation as a weather forecaster. We have already seen that storms were attributed to planetary conjunctions so it is no surprise that the astrologer should be thought

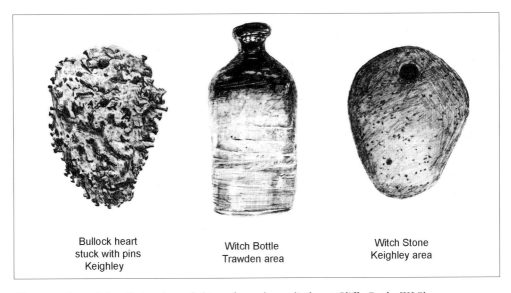

Bullock heart
stuck with pins
Keighley

Witch Bottle
Trawden area

Witch Stone
Keighley area

Charms against witchcraft, drawings of objects formerly on display at Cliffe Castle. [KLS]

Acton Street – Jack Kay's house was the one on the right-hand end of the row, *c.* 1960.

Rush Isles, 1964. This, the older of two buildings at Rush Isles, is now in ruins. [HH/KLS]

able to predict (and possibly to control) the weather. This aspect of his work is remembered in Bill o'th' Hoylus End's *History o' Haworth Railway* when it is debated whether the first sod should be dug 'next muck-spreading toime' or on 'gert wind day in't memory o' Oud Jack Kay'. Either way it is suggested that were Jack still alive the railway would probably have been built to somewhere other than Keighley on the grounds that 'Keighla is not worthy of amalgamashun wi' a rispectable city like Haworth.'

John Kay was baptised at St Michael's in Haworth in 1766, married a woman called Rebecca (her surname is uncertain – there were four marriages of men called John Kay to women called Rebecca between 1785 and 1791) around 1790 and had three or four children. Descendants of his son Thomas are still living in Yorkshire. Kay is variously described as a weaver or a butcher in the parish records but his death certificate calls him a soothsayer. He died at the age of eighty in 1847 at his house in Acton Street off North Street where he is said to have lived 'upwards of forty years'. The house was demolished around 1970 and the site is now a car park.

Where Jack Kay depended upon magic to effect his cures, the horse doctors of Rush Isles made use of more tangible medicaments to cure man and beast. The list is long, colourful, imaginatively spelled (and not a little emetic): green of(f) a coper cetel, tood spawn or slubber, French flies powder'd, opodeldoc, burnt spunge, one scruple millepede, cinneber of antimony (these three all in one recipe), corrocive sublemate, whick worms, sucatellus balsum, the urine of a red cow, black snails. These ingredients and many more are specified in recipes in the Rush Isles commonplace -book. This manuscript was written between 1787 and 1842 by a number of hands at Rush Isles Farm near Ponden. The chief compiler was William Heaton who wrote his contributions around 1800. Amongst various business and family records and the astrological chart mentioned above are hundreds of recipes. These comprise cures for various ailments of men, horses and cows and a number of useful preparations for a variety of other purposes. Horses can be cured of pole evil, spavin, mad staggers, sweld legs, mange, quitters, broken knees and bellewark. Cows can be treated for flux, gripes or hoose, foul in feet, cripple felon, milk fever and blond water. They can be made to take a bull and the bull, should the need arise, can be treated for clap. The bull had to be thrown on his back, his pizzle drawn from its sheath and rubbed with stamped house leek and blue milk – the Rush Isles farmers were obviously hardy men. The bull must also be dosed with cream of tartar, jalap and calomel. The poisonous nature of this concoction is hinted at: 'if the beast be badly with the medicine give him a pint of sweet oil to correct it.'

There are as many treatments for the ailments of man as for cows and horses put together, although in some cases it is not clear which species is meant and some recipes are said to be good 'for Man or Beast'. One could be treated for blasts, rewmatick, hooping cough, childblains, itch, eruptive fever, leperese, inflamshun, fitts, scurvy, consumption, Darby neck or for cancer – amongst many other ills. Some medicines are named: green bottle, red bottle, dyat drink, wound water and the salves – black, white and green.

Some of the ingredients have already been mentioned above but a closer look might be of interest. They may be divided into four main groups: chemical, herbal, animal and ordinary foodstuffs. The last named including milk, ale, treacle, hogs lard, eggs and honey are mainly used as vehicles for the active ingredients. The animal medicines strike us as the most odd: live worms, toad spawn and black snails (i.e. slugs). The patients were probably grateful for the fact that these were, in the main, applied externally. Urine was made use of in medicine – as it was in a very wide variety of applications. The fact that old urine was specified suggests that the ammonia content was what was wanted. A prescription involving the urine of a red cow for cancers is inexplicable – and no doubt ineffectual (although we are told that if it does not work the application must be repeated). French flies are indicated to make a cow take the bull – French fly is cantharides or Spanish fly which has a long-standing reputation as an aphrodisiac.

The array of chemical and herbal ingredients available in this remote country district around 1800 is impressive. Since the disappearance of true chemists' shops over the last few decades one simply could not buy most of these ingredients today. In the case of some of the chemicals used this is probably not a bad thing. Copper, lead and mercury compounds are all enthusiastically prescribed and all are poisonous. Other chemicals specified are less toxic and might have had some beneficial effect – sulphur, cream of tartar, sal ammoniac, alum, Glauber's salt and various oils amongst them.

The herbal ingredients are largely exotic, including as they do, galangal, ginger, fenugreek, rhubarb (medicinal, not the garden variety), dragon's blood, elecampane, frankincense, myrrh and opium. Some might have been grown in the herb garden: sage, rue, fennel, bay, vervain and camomile. Finally there were those plants which might have been found growing locally: wild carrot, aniseed, horse mint, juniper, St John's Wort, tormentil, whortle berry and dog standers. The last named might sound unfamiliar but it is a very common plant – ragwort. It is interesting to note that there is a Dog Stander Field in the Sladen Valley at no great distance from Rush Isles.

As well as all these cures for the ailments of men, cows and horses there are numerous 'workshop receipts' as the Victorians would later call them. These embrace stains and varnishes (including an invaluable green varnish for spitting boxes), inks, glue, shoe blacking and various wines. There are methods for removing stains and cleaning such diverse materials as silver plate, marble, linen, feathers, paintings and gilded frames. You may learn how to gild glass or brass, silver metals, plate copper or Japan tin. You can also case-harden gun locks, stain gun stocks, preserve peas, destroy caterpillars or fuddle fish. This last operation involves casting chopped worms soaked in brandy on the water. The fish rise to take the worms, get drunk on the brandy and fall prey to the waiting fish-fuddler's net.

One recipe in the book has its title heavily obliterated. This is an account of the process for making malt. The reason for this caution is to be found in a later entry for ' a certain cure for Darby neck'. This involves sprouting and roasting barley – 'not for Malt but for Medicinal use'. After the barley has been sprouted it is to be dried in a 'Drying Ciln if you dare for fear of the Excise men fining you'. Presumably William Heaton had recently had an unpleasant encounter with the excise men.

It seems most probable that Heaton made at least part of his living from his medical activities. He is described as a surgeon in the parish registers in 1801. We know that he paid for some of his recipes – as much as £2 in one case. The ingredients for his recipes must have taken much effort and expense to acquire. He was quite well-off – he had the farm at Rush Isles, received rents for other properties and, in 1799, got £300 for his share in the Ponden cotton mill. Heaton most likely acted as doctor and vet to the surrounding farms and villages besides running his own farm. One thing is certain – all his recipes could not stave off his death of a decline at the age of forty-one in 1810.

ten

The Brontës' Haworth

Undoubtedly Haworth's greatest fame is its association with the Brontë family. The writings of Anne, Charlotte and Emily Brontë have a large and devoted clan of readers and the story of their lives fascinates many more. This story has been told often, sometimes well and sometimes not so well. To summarise it here would be pointless, but there are aspects of the Brontë family's relationship with Haworth and its people which are less well known and worth investigating. For all their achievements in literature, the Brontë sisters had little influence on the Haworth of their day – nor could they have had given the nature of society at the time. Since their deaths, however, they have wrought great changes in the village. Without them Haworth would not have become a place of literary pilgrimage and would bear a very different face today: no Brontë Museum, fewer summer tourists and the shops, cafés and guest houses cater for them. At the same time, though, there would be fewer facilities for those who live here. Not all the shops which serve the residents could survive without the extra trade from tourism, and there would be fewer pubs and restaurants and, possibly, even less public transport.

Posthumous influence apart, it was Patrick Brontë of all his family who had the greatest impact on the village to which he came in 1820. Apart from his principal role as perpetual curate, Patrick took an enlightened interest in the wellbeing of his parishioners. He was not afraid of offending the wealthier residents if he thought that the ordinary people were being neglected or ill-treated. One might cite his support for the 1833 Factory Act which sought to regulate the employment of children in the mills. Patrick was also in favour of moderate Parliamentary reform – if only to stave off the risk of revolution. He was vehemently opposed to the barbarity of the 1834 Poor Law, the aim of which was to drive the poor into the workhouse – and to make it as unpleasant as possible. The Haworth Poor Law Guardians resigned in protest against the new Act. A statement supporting their decision, which was signed by Patrick and other leading citizens, expressed their 'most decided abhorrence of the unjust, tyrannical, unconstitutional and unintelligible Act'.

Perhaps Brontë's greatest contribution to the welfare of his parishioners was his struggle to get the provisions of the Public Health Act of 1848 applied in Haworth. It was in large part due to Patrick's efforts that Babbage was sent to Haworth to report on its sanitary condition. Without Patrick, Haworth would almost certainly not have had a Local Board of Health anywhere near so early as 1851. Some of the wealthier inhabitants were strongly opposed to such moves to improve water supply and sewage disposal facilities in Haworth as they would have to pay for works that would mostly benefit others. Brontë overrode their objections and ensured that a start was made in the daunting task of rendering Haworth a decent and healthy place for people to live.

Patrick was served by many local people in a variety of capacities during his time in Haworth. These have not always been adequately dealt with by Brontë scholars and it might be well to set out here what we know of some of them.

First comes Joseph Redman who was Patrick's parish clerk for thirty-six years. Redman was born at Rough Nook, on the road to Stanbury, in 1796, the third of the seven children of John Redman a wool-comber and his wife Peggy. Joseph married Betty Ogden in 1817 and they had eight children between 1817 and 1833. Redman started his working life as a weaver but advanced to the post of parish clerk around 1826. He and Betty started their married life at Rough Nook with Joseph's parents but were living in their own house in the Fold by 1841. He was to live there for the rest of his life. For one who played a large part in the life of the church and the village for nearly forty years, we know very little about Redman. He starts appearing as a regular witness at marriages in 1819 and acts in this capacity frequently from 1826 until 1862 – a good indicator of a close association with the church. He was one of the few present at the wedding of Charlotte Brontë and Arthur Bell Nicholls. There is a recollection preserved of his being summoned from his house when the wedding party was about to leave the parsonage. It is said that he stopped to tie his bootlace on his way to the church – an astonishingly minute detail to know from a life of which we otherwise know so little.

He handled the correspondence with the Board of Health in London and when the Local Board was established he was appointed its clerk at a salary of £17 a year. It seems that he made his living largely from the two posts of parish clerk and clerk to the Local Board although he is described as an architect around 1850. He acted as architect when the new bells were put in the church tower in 1846.

His first wife died in 1856 and later in the same year he married Nelly Maud, a widow.

An indication of his closeness to Patrick Brontë is the fact that he was one of the witnesses to Patrick's will in 1855. He survived Patrick by a little over a year, dying in July 1862. His widow Nelly was paid the £8 which was owing to him in wages from the Local Board (his salary had risen to £30 p.a.) and was also paid 5s for cleaning the Board's offices. She lived on for a further twenty-two years, dying in 1884.

When Patrick Brontë arrived in Haworth his sexton was William Brown, who had already held the post for thirteen years under the incumbency of James Charnock. William is said to have lived in Changegate – then known as Ginnel. He was born around 1780, the son of John Brown. He married Mary Bowcock in 1803 and their son John was born the following year. Three further children followed over the next seven years. William died in 1835 and Mary three years later

– both were in their fifties. On the very day that William died in 1835, his son John was appointed to succeed him as sexton. John is thought to have built the house in Church Street known as Sexton House some time in the 1830s. John's marriage to his wife Mary is not recorded in the Haworth registers but their children's baptisms are. They probably married around 1823 and their first child Sarah was born in 1824. Sarah died in infancy but a further six daughters were born between 1826 and 1841. A son, John William, who was born and died in 1838, is mentioned on the family gravestone but is not in the parish registers – presumably the child died at birth. The Brown daughters who are remembered as servants of the Brontë family were Martha, Eliza and Tabitha, who were born in 1828, 1831 and 1834 respectively. Neither John nor his father William was dependent upon the small income which they drew as church sexton – each of them was also a stone mason. No doubt much of the monumental work in Haworth would come their way.

One of John Brown's main interests outside his business was the Masonic Lodge of the Three Graces. He joined in 1830 and was Worshipful Master of the Lodge by 1832. Brown went on to hold that post for a remarkable total of thirteen years over the next twenty-three years. It was John Brown who introduced Patrick's son Branwell to the lodge. Special dispensation was granted for Branwell to enter the lodge under the usual age – he was only nineteen. He does not seem to have been a particularly exemplary member of the lodge – being described as 'more of a warning than an ornament to the Craft'. It is, of course, largely for his association with Branwell – particularly in his drinking exploits, that John Brown is remembered today. A number of contemporary commentators clearly thought that Brown led Branwell astray – although one doubts if he took much leading. John Brown died in 1855 and was succeeded as sexton by his younger brother William – the last man to hold that post. As already mentioned, three of John Brown's daughters acted as servants at the parsonage. Eliza and Tabitha helped out occasionally when required but Martha became a full-time servant of the Brontës after Tabitha Aykroyd was disabled by a fall. Martha Brown was a servant at the parsonage from around 1839 until Patrick's death in 1861. She then went to Ireland with Arthur Nicholls but returned to Haworth the

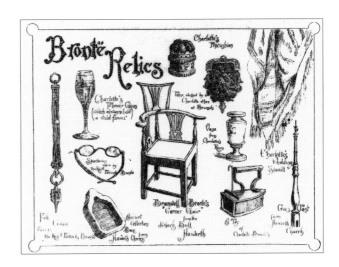

Objects from the Browns' Brontë Museum, *c.* 1890. [KLS]

following year. She died in a cottage at Ducking Well (on Sun Street) in 1880. Some years after Martha's death two of her cousins, Robinson and Francis Brown, opened a museum of Brontë relics at 123 Main Street. Some of the artefacts displayed had come to them through the family. Their museum opened in 1889, which was unfortunate timing – the flow of tourists was apparently much diminished following the demolition of the old church. Their collection was auctioned off in 1898.

Tabitha Aykroyd, who was the senior servant at the parsonage, is something of an enigma. The story of her devotion to the Brontë family is well known. She came to the parsonage in 1825 and stayed there for the rest of her life. In a fall in the street in December 1836 she suffered a badly fractured leg which immobilised her for a long period and limited her activity for the rest of her days. It is well known that the Brontë girls would not countenance her removal from the parsonage and insisted that they must care for her as she had cared for them. 'Tabby' did eventually leave for a couple of years, going to live with her sister Susannah Wood in 1839 and returning to the parsonage in 1842.

During these years Tabitha and her sister were living in a cottage belonging to their younger relative William Wood on Newell Hill (now Lodge Street) off Main Street.

This may well have been one of three cottages which Tabitha and William Wood had jointly bought in 1836. After returning to the parsonage in 1842 Tabitha remained there until shortly before her death in 1855. Her last days were spent at the home of William Wood's sister Mary Ratcliffe. It was Mary's husband Benjamin Ratcliffe who registered Tabitha's death which took place at his home, Follyfield House. This is now Nos 41 and 43 Sun Street. I said above that Tabitha was an enigma. It is very difficult to know exactly who she was. We know that she was Susannah Wood's sister and she is usually said to have been William Wood's aunt. An oft-repeated story is that she spent some years working on a farm in Lancashire, was married, widowed and then returned to Haworth where she went to work at the parsonage. However a deed has come to light which unequivocally describes her as a single woman and calls her 'Miss Akroyd'. No trace can be found of any baptism for her or her sister or the George Aykroyd with whom they are buried. This might be explained by the assertion that she was a Methodist. It is clear that she was closely related to William Wood but the details remain obscure despite considerable efforts to clarify the matter.

Tabby's relative William Wood lived in a largish house on Newell Hill (now Lodge Street) where he conducted his trade as a carpenter and joiner. Above the door of his house may still be seen a 'taking in door' which served his first-floor workshop. Through this door would have passed, one after another, the coffins in which the Brontës were laid to rest. He made coffins in great variety at prices ranging from 1s 2d to £2 4s – his bill for Branwell's funeral was £3 15s. He did many mundane jobs for the Brontës – making small pieces of furniture and carrying out all manner of minor repairs at the parsonage. There is a story that Charlotte once persuaded him to accept three of Branwell's paintings in payment for a mirror on which she had set her heart. Of his bargain he said, 'I felt like a fool as I came down the lane with three pictures not worth a sixpence instead of the brass I expected.' After Branwell and Charlotte were both dead he came to value them more highly and refused all offers to purchase them.

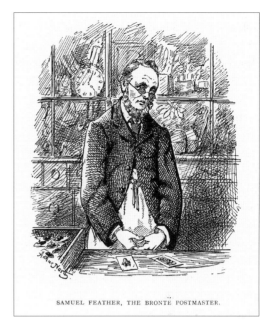

SAMUEL FEATHER, THE BRONTË POSTMASTER.

Above left: William Wood's house, Lodge Street. The door through which the Brontës' coffins would have come is on the second floor above the steps. [SCW]

Above right: 'Samuel Feather' from Meeker's *Haworth, Home of the Brontës*, 1895.

Another tradesman who features prominently in the Brontë biographies is the stationer John Greenwood. His devotion to the Brontë family and his dedication to their memory are well known – as is his controversial decision to name one of his sons Brontë Greenwood. The baptism of this child was the very last performed by Patrick and the cause of strife between him and his son-in-law Nicholls. Stories are told of Greenwood walking to Halifax and back to buy half a ream of paper so as not to disappoint Haworth's budding authors. It has been claimed that his shop was next to the church steps but it is beyond dispute that in 1851 his shop and house were at what is now 36 Main Street. An apparent complication is that his descendants believe that his shop was at 78 Main Street. An examination of the census returns shows that he did move to that part of Main Street between 1851 and 1861 and so the difficulty is resolved.

The shop beside the church steps at the top of Main Street (No. 121) was, in fact, the post office. Again the whereabouts of the post office and the identity of the postmaster during the Brontë period has been the subject of conflicting claims. A detailed study of the trade directories and other sources show William Hartley was the postmaster at 121 Main Street between 1834 and 1854 – and probably longer. Sometime between 1854 and 1861 Edwin Feather took over the job and the post office moved to his shop at the other end of the same row – i.e. 125 Main Street. Claude Meeker's claim in his *Haworth; Home of the Brontës* that Samuel Feather was the postmaster who handled the Brontë manuscripts is, at first sight, rather odd. There was no one of that name in Haworth in any of the census returns. Later Meeker corrects the name to *Edwin*

Feather, who was a watchmaker at 125 Main Street at the time of Meeker's visit and who had been the postmaster – but not until the mid-1850s at the earliest. Meeker's portrait of Feather 'the Brontë postmaster' is irresistible and is reproduced here.

Finally I must mention Joseph Hardaker the apothecary. Hardaker has already been mentioned in Chapter 7 where I speculated about the possibility that Robert Lambert had taken over his chemist's shop. The truth is that we do not know where Hardaker's shop was – like Tabitha Aykroyd he is an elusive character. He was born in 1790 at Lees, near Haworth, the son of a poor wool-comber. His health was poor, his constitution weak and he never married. He was reputed to be an able, intelligent, self-educated man with many interests. He is said to have opened the first chemist's shop in Haworth and to have been patronised by the Brontës and other notable Haworth residents 'more for his native talents and evident intellectual superiority than for the meagre accommodation his shop afforded'. He apparently tried most brands of religion and ended up a Roman Catholic. Hardaker was also a writer, somewhat less well known than the Brontës maybe, but he did publish three books of verse between 1822 and 1831. His verse is very much of its time and would not appeal to many modern readers. There are one or two interesting references to Haworth amongst his poems. In *To the Sexton* he castigates that official as a hypocrite and a drunkard:

> Oft have we seen you humming, throng,
> Some fav'rite Bachanalian song;
> Or whistling while ye hack'd among
> The mould'ring few;
> Oft have ye fractur'd skulls, whom long
> In life ye knew.

If the lines are aimed at William Brown, who was sexton at that time, they cannot have done anything to improve relations between the two men.

Hardaker clearly did not think much of conviviality as we may see from his *Tour to Bolton Abbey*. He describes how he set out to walk to Bolton Abbey 'To shun the clamours of each vulgar brute', explaining in a footnote, 'It was Haworth Fair'.

Some of his titles are more memorable than his verse: *To a Worm which the Author had nearly trod on*, *An Epistle of Condolence to my Lady's Lap-Dog Pompey* and *To the Author's fine Collection of Walking-Sticks or Bundle of Crutches*. These are all from *Poems Lyric and Moral*, 1822. His last published work was *The Bridal of Tomar*, 1831 which is distinctly unmemorable. In between came his rarest work – and most wonderful title: *The Aeropteron or Steam-Carriage*, 1830. This is an account of the opening of the Liverpool & Manchester Railway. The title page and accompanying illustration are delightful and are reproduced here. Joseph Hardaker died in 1840 and one writer states that he is buried in Haworth churchyard but there is no record of his burial in the registers.

And with that we come to the end of this brief look at the Brontës' Haworth – but who is this knocking impetuously at the door of my book as I am about to close it?

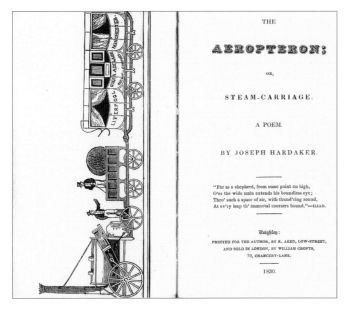

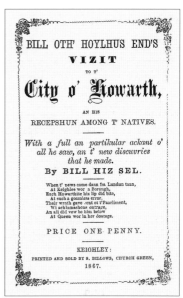

Above left: Title page of Joseph Hardaker's *The Aeropteron*, 1830. [KLS]

Above right: Title page of Bill o' th' Hoylus End's *Vizit to t' City of Haworth*, 1867.

A rough-looking cove, and none too sober I fear, but he is not to be refused – come in Bill, and welcome. Bill o' th' Hoylus End has been quoted more than once in these pages and he shall close them. William Wright was born in 1836 at Hoylus End just outside Haworth Township on the way to Keighley. The house is long since demolished but it stood on Hainworth Crag Road at what was then Hermit Hole (Hermit Hole has, for reasons best known to itself, moved down the road towards Keighley since Bill's time).

The tale of Bill's life is long and colourful and would make another book, but what matters here is that he was a very good writer of dialect verse and humorous prose. He had a long, somewhat picaresque association with Haworth and his tales of tobacco-chewing monkeys and South American war pigs are not quite forgotten yet. He wrote much on Haworth, including the very scarce *Vizit to t' City o' Howarth* and a downright scurrilous broadsheet on the demolition of the old church entitled *Haworth Church, the Bronté's Shrine an't Parson's Kleptomania*, but we will close with his incomparable description of Haworth from his *History o' Haworth Railway*:

Haworth is a city at's little nawn, if onny, in th' history o' Ingland, tho thare's no daat but it's as oud as Methuslam, if net ouder, yet wi' being built so far aat o' th' latitude o' civilised nashuns, nobody's scarcely nawn owt abaat it wal lately. Th' faanders of it is sed to be people fra th' Eastern countries, for they tuk fearful after em in Haworth i'th line o'soothsayers, magishuns, an' istralegers ; but whether they cum fra th' East or th' West, thay luk oud fasun'd enuff … Sum foak sez it wur th' last place 'at wur made, but it's a mistak, for it looks oud fashun'd enuff to be th' first 'at wur made.

Sources and Further Reading

It is not possible to indicate all the sources which have been drawn upon, but much of this book was based upon extensive research in local archives – mainly those at Keighley Local Studies Library.

There are a number of important books which will extend the reader's knowledge of Haworth Township. The newer ones also contain detailed bibliographies.

Amongst the older books are:

J. Horsfall Turner, *Haworth, Past and Present*, 1879.
Joseph Craven, *A Brontë Moorland Village and its People : A History of Stanbury*, 1907.

Recent and forthcoming books of importance are:

Kenneth Emsley, *Historic Haworth Today*, 1995.
Robin Greenwood, *A History of the Greenwoods of Haworth* (10 vols), unpublished
  MS, 1999.
Robin Greenwood, *Haworth's Landowners, Mills and Millowners and other Principal
  Families during the Brontë Era, 1820-61*, unpublished MS, 2002.
Dennis Thompson, *Stanbury, A Pennine Country Village*, 2002.
Reg Hindley, *Oxenhope, the Making of a Pennine Community*, 2004.
Reg Hindley, *Oxenhope, an introduction in Nine Guided Walks*, due 2005.
Michael Baumber, *The Rise and Fall of a Textile Community, Haworth Oxenhope &
  Stanbury from the Earliest Times to 1974*, due 2006.

Index